HUMVEE

Bill Munro

The Crowood Press

First published in 2002 by
The Crowood Press Ltd
Ramsbury, Marlborough
Wiltshire SN8 2HR

www.crowood.com

British Library Cataloguing–in–Publication Data
A catalogue record for this book is available from the British Library.

ISBN 1 86126 532 8

Photographic Acknowledgements
The author is grateful to the following for their help in supplying the pictures in this book.
Dave Ahl; Mark Askew; Jim Calhoun; Jeff Ciccione; Fred Crismon; Shaun C. Connors; Dodmedia, the US Department of Defense image service; Sean Gosling; Burt Mead; Albert Mroz; C.B. Stevens; Richard Stickland; Tony Sudds: TACOM; Pat Ware; Cyd Williams.

Typeface used: Bembo.

Typeset and designed by
D & N Publishing
Baydon, Marlborough, Wiltshire.

Printed and bound in Great Britain by Bookcraft, Midsomer Norton.

Contents

Introduction

It is all a matter of logistics. Napoleon Bonaparte is credited with saying, 'An army marches on its stomach.' The logical extension of that observation is that, whoever you are going to fight, wherever you are going to fight him, you need to keep your troops supplied not with food alone, but with enough equipment to get the job done. And for the maximum of effect you need to get the equipment to them with the minimum of effort and complication. As far as the vehicles used for fighting and for support are concerned, that can encompass as big or small a quantity and type as the people responsible for the job deem necessary. Naturally, a Jeep will not do the job of a 5-ton truck nor vice versa, but a truck with a capacity of 1ton or thereabouts can be adapted to several roles, and that is where the HMMWV, the Humvee or the Hummer, as it came to be known, comes in. An old maxim says, 'Compromises are rarely satisfactory.' If the Humvee is a compromise, then it is the rare exception that has indeed proved more than satisfactory: it has in most cases proved to be greater than the sum of its parts.

In attempting to develop a vehicle that would take over the roles of others as varied as the little M151 MUTT, the conventional Dodge M880 and the oddball Gama Goat then, as the song says, 'Something's gotta give.' Or at least it ought to. If, so to speak, anything did, it was the vehicle's width. In trying to get the ground clearance essential for good off-road performance, still retain as low a centre of gravity as possible and offer an optimum of load capacity the Humvee had to be wide. It was no longer and barely higher than its civilian Senior Jeep cousins, the Wagoneer and J-Series trucks, but at 84in (213cm) it was at least 8in (20cm) wider. Compared with the M151's 62in (157cm) and the 70in (178cm) of

the M37 Dodge of the 1950s, it does not seem quite so broad in the beam, but alongside its contemporaries, the M35 2½-ton truck and the huge Oshkosh HEMTT (Heavy Expanded Mobility Tactical Truck), both 94in (239cm) wide, the Humvee looks skinny. However, it would fit into the aircraft that would deploy it to a battle zone, the CH47 Chinook helicopter, and that is what mattered.

The stability given by that width, coupled with permanent four-wheel drive and a big V8 diesel engine, endowed the Humvee with unparalleled off-road performance. There are stories from Jeep owners in off-road trail events, such as those run in the Moab Desert in the USA, who have recalled that they simply stared in disbelief as a civilian Hummer made nothing of some hill or virtual cliff that they, with their much modified vehicles, could not even dream of driving over. It is no wonder that the Humvee, or Hummer, earned the epithet 'Jeep on steroids'.

In military service it was natural that shortcomings would be found that could not be foreseen in testing. Extra armour was one addition after casualties were suffered in Somalia, and the Heavy Hummer Variant was developed when the original model's suspension was not up to the job of carrying a shelter or towing an artillery piece. It is to the designers' credit that these difficulties were overcome with straightforward, bolt-on modifications. It must have been gratifying for them to know that they had got it right first time.

A Word about Names

Very seldom, if ever, has a vehicle been made that has been known concurrently by more than one name. It is also extremely rare for an unofficial name to become the official one, as in the case of the jeep. It was Willys-Overland, the makers of the production World War II jeep who, after a protracted legal battle, won the right to use the name Jeep as a brand name for their civilian models. The subject of this book has no fewer than three names, and it is appropriate that some explanation should given as to how and why they arose, and how they will be used here. From the outset, the US military gave the XM998 programme the title HMMWV, standing for High Mobility Multipurpose Wheeled Vehicle. Unlike HEMTT or MUTT, this was unpronounceable and the letters soon became slurred into the more user-friendly 'Humvee'. This name was shortened still further to 'Hummer'. AM General, the makers of the vehicle chosen for production, were a part of the American Motors Corporation, which at the time owned the Jeep brand name. They were naturally aware of their own history and quickly registered the word 'Hummer' as a brand name.

In 1993 AM General produced a civilian version of the vehicle, sold under the name 'Hummer'. When AM General decided that servicing civilian dealerships was not entirely compatible with their core business of building vehicles for the government, they sold the marketing rights, along with the brand name, to someone with far more experience in automotive marketing: General Motors. In using the brand name, GM adopted their own protocol, spelling the name HUMMER, and always in capital letters.

Therefore we have three names and two ways of expressing one of them: HMMWV, Humvee, Hummer and HUMMER, and we shall use them thus: 'HMMWV' will be used in the early chapters when dealing with all vehicles submitted to the US military under the procurement programme. For clarity, the name will be linked with that of the relevant manufacturer, that is, Teledyne, Chrysler, General Dynamics or AM General; 'Humvee' will be used when referring to all the production military vehicles built by AM General (an exception will be the HHV, the Heavy Hummer Variant, a name given by AM General when they had the rights to the name); Humvee is also a registered trade mark of AM General; 'Hummer' will be used when dealing with the civilian vehicles made and marketed by AM General; and 'HUMMER' will be used in reference to the models marketed by General Motors.

Acknowledgements

The author thanks the following for their assistance in the production of this book.

From official bodies: United States Department of Defense; Department of Public Information, United Nations; Randy R. Talbot and Ann M. Bos, TACOM; the Defense Attaché, American Embassy, London; DTLR Vehicle Standards and Engineering Division; and the Studebaker Museum.

From the auto and defence industries: Craig McNab, Lee Woodward and Rob Wurtz of AM General; Nancy Kaza and Paul Beckett of GM Hummer Division; Heinz König of Motorwagenfabrik AG; and Vivian Van Brienen of General Dynamic Land Systems.

Military vehicle enthusiasts and fellow writers: Mark Askew; Jim Calhoun; Andrew Camp; Richard Coussé; Shaun C. Connors; John Dowdeswell of Brooklands Books; Kit Foster; Rod Foster; Virginia Hirons of czbrats; Roger Jerram; Ian McLean; S.J. Payne; Derek Redmond; Mark Robinson; C.B. Stevens; Richard Stickland; Gordon Toy; Pat Ware; Ken Whowell; and Cyd Williams.

Special thanks go to Patrick Kear and Dale Johnson for their assistance in getting this project off the ground, and to Albert Mroz for his help and enthusiasm throughout. If I have forgotten anyone, then please forgive me.

1 The Roots of the Humvee

World War II brought the USA out of its self-imposed political isolation for good. The Korean War, the conflict in Vietnam and the Cold War established the USA as the most powerful nation on the planet, the major partner, or opponent, in any conflict, large or small, wherever in the world it might occur. Thus, in either defending its sovereign territory or fulfilling its obligations under the UN or NATO banner, the USA's military requirements are for hardware that can serve in any climate, in any country, and can be shipped as easily and as quickly as possible.

Transportability and ease of maintenance are vital to the military, and that means as much standardization as possible. Coupled to that, each class of vehicle, armoured and soft-skinned, must fulfil its role to the best possible level given the technology of its time. In recent times the US military sought to develop a range of vehicles that met just those requirements and that vehicle materialized as the HMMWV. In it they have a standardized light vehicle that is the base of a truck, a weapons carrier, a troop carrier, a shelter carrier and an ambulance. The path towards this standardization, as part of a constant drive to update and improve to meet the ever-changing demands made on the US military, has wound its way over seventy troubled years. However, the desire to mechanize the Army of a country that grew up with the automobile began before the Great War. As part of the HMMWV's history let us look at the development of the American light military truck, as shaped by history.

A New Army

At the end of the nineteenth century the US Army was not in good condition. Following the horrors of the Civil War, the American people turned their back on the idea of war. The Army's main tasks in the latter half of that century had been to drive the Native Americans from their homelands to make way for settlers, and, for all too brief a time, to safeguard the emancipation of slaves in the defeated Confederate States. But a number of Republican Congressmen believed that America should be as influential as Britain in administering 'uncivilized' parts of the globe. The government's thrust for trade across the Pacific towards China and south to Latin America demanded, and got, a much-improved Navy. By 1898 the USA had gained Hawaii, in 1899 it annexed part of the Samoan Islands and had taken control of the Philippines by 1902. But the Spanish–American War of 1898, begun to protect American trade interests in Cuba, showed the dire condition of the Army and its organization.

Cuba at this time was a Spanish colony, but the repressed population staged a revolt against a brutal new governor and the USA provided support. The most famous stories from the Spanish-American War are of the storming of San Juan Hill and of Theodore Roosevelt and his Roughriders. But, although just 379 American soldiers died in battle in the whole war, more than 5,000 died through malnutrition and disease in their own camps. Major steps had to be taken to improve the administration of the Army and prevent such disasters happening again.

Pershing in Mexico

By the time of the American involvement in Mexico between 1914 and 1917 under Gen John

'Black Jack' Pershing, the US Army was much smarter, better organized and better equipped. One innovation was the quick acquisition of a number of Dodge touring cars, which Pershing used to chase the Mexican revolutionary Pancho Villa across Mexico after he had the temerity to raid American sovereign territory. While the idea of using the Dodges was good in principle, they were less than reliable and Pershing learned a lot from the experience.

In 1910, even before Pershing's encounter with Villa, some form of light, fast and manoeuvrable reconnaissance vehicle to replace the cavalryman's horse had been envisaged. An essential part of horsemanship is the bond created between horse and rider, and the cavalryman, while accepting that his horse is as much a 'soldier' as himself, feels deep regret when his mount is injured or killed in action. Thus the cavalry would welcome anything that would spare a horse distress. Motorcycles were tried for scouting duties but were still crude and underpowered, and so the Army began to consider automobiles. In a trial in 1910 the Model T Ford and the 20hp Hupmobile came out best, but neither was ideal.

The USA Goes to War

German U-boat activity in the Great War, sinking the liner *Lusitania* and much other shipping, had tested the patience of the US government and people, but moves to push the country into military action had been resisted. Indeed, many American citizens were of recent German descent and favoured siding with the Kaiser. However, the Zimmerman telegram intercepted by US Intelligence in January 1917 revealed a plot by Germany to help Mexico to regain territory it lost to the USA in 1840. This was the last straw for President Woodrow Wilson, who persuaded Congress to pass a declaration of war on Germany on 2 April 1917.

It took America a long time to mobilize: there were not nearly enough men in uniform and little in the way of suitable hardware. By the time Gen Pershing had his Army made ready to fight in the summer of 1918, the Germans were about to break the deadlock of trench warfare with their use of storm troops. Fighting in the French sector of the Western Front, American troops – Doughboys, as they called themselves – were engaged in more open conflict than had been seen in the previous three and a half years. Seeing the sheer potential of America's fighting force, its wealth and the freshness of the men on the ground, the Germans, by now totally drained and experiencing mutiny within their armed forces and civil unrest at home, sued for peace.

(Incidentally, no one knows for sure how the American troops got their nickname of 'doughboys'. One, perhaps too obvious explanation comes from an association with the name of Woodrow Wilson's Secretary of War, Newton D. Baker. The origin of another is a little earlier, coming from the Mexican campaign. The houses in Mexico were built of hard-baked red clay bricks known as *adobes*. Many of the American troops came from the colder north. Burnt red as adobes by the sun, they were nicknamed 'adobe boys', soon corrupted to 'doughboys'.)

Four-Wheel Drive

The invention of a universal joint by Otto Zachow and William Besserditch in Wisconsin in the first year of the twentieth century had enabled them to build a four-wheel-drive steam truck. This vehicle was not successful, but in 1911 their Four Wheel Drive Automobile Company (also known as FWD) was making petrol-engined trucks with drive to all four wheels. The US Army tested one, liked it and by the end of the Great War had bought some 15,000. Thomas B. Jeffery was another automobile pioneer who, after producing the Rambler light car, entered truck manufacture in 1914. He too built a four-wheel-drive truck, named the Quad, which was adopted by the US Army's Quartermaster Corps in 1913 as the Army's first 1-ton vehicle.

Both the FWD and the Quad proved their worth in the mud of France, alongside two-wheel-drive makes such as the Mack and Autocar. With its simplicity and ease of maintenance,

This beautifully restored 1918 FWD was first used by the US Army in France in World War I.

the Model T Ford proved invaluable in the role of light truck and ambulance, as did General Motors' light and medium trucks and the new ½-ton Dodge. The lack of experience of the US Army with motor vehicles – and they were not alone in this – was no brake on their inventiveness. The simplicity of the vehicles and the readily available craft skills of the troops saw trucks quickly adapted to serve the needs of individual units. Bodies were adapted, guns mounted, weather protection fitted. Motorcycles had improved by this time and Harley Davidson and Excelsior models, many fitted with sidecars mounting light machine-guns, served as weapons carriers and light reconnaissance machines. But with over 200 makes of vehicle in service, servicing was a nightmare for the motor pools. The Class B Liberty Truck was the

US Army's first attempt at producing its own vehicle. It was not a success: it was extremely expensive to develop and, by the time it was ready, it was already outdated.

At Peace Again

Between the two World Wars America returned to the isolationist policy it had pursued after the Civil War, and its military were restricted to domestic duties and the country's interests in the Pacific and the Caribbean. As regards transportation, the Army had to make do with vehicles left over from the Great War, even though the country prospered through most of the 1920s. What vehicles the Army had were supplemented by a small number of new, civilian vehicles. In 1933

This 1918 Model T Ford illustrates the kind of light vehicle used by the US Army in World War I. The machine gun would have been installed by the troops who operated the truck. All kinds of adaptations like this were made in the field: there was no real experience in using motorized vehicles from which the Quartermaster Corps or any other part of the Army could draw to give guidance as to what might be required. Incidentally, the 'X' in the number indicates that it was a civilian vehicle commandeered by the Army.

the War Department decided to purchase 'complete vehicles from the automotive industry'. Procurement for US Army vehicles was then the responsibility of two separate corps. The Ordnance Department took care of combat vehicles – tanks and such like – while the Quartermaster Corps were responsible for general-purpose vehicles. The QMC divided these into administrative types, based on regular civilian vehicles, and specifically-designed or adapted tactical types, which were used for combat support.

A Light Weapons Carrier

The US Army's search for a light reconnaissance vehicle continued with an investigation of tracked vehicles and a reappraisal of the Ford T, but neither produced a satisfactory result. The

Austin Seven had been in use in the 1920s by the British Army as a scout car, and French and German armed forces used licence-built versions in a similar role. In 1929 Herbert Austin began building the Seven in America in a factory in Butler, Pennsylvania. The idea of using an ultra-light vehicle for reconnaissance duties had yet to be explored by the US Army. However, they tried an American-built Austin Seven in 1932, but discarded it.

The concept of a light weapons carrier was pursued by Col Robert G. Howie, who had been an infantry officer in France in the Great War and thus realized the importance of deploying machine-guns to hold ground won by the infantry in battle. But he had been connected with motor vehicles all his life, and began experimenting with civilian vehicles to try and evaluate what was

The T215 Dodge in WC58 command car guise. Note how narrow the track is in comparison with the later weapons carrier and ambulance on pages 16 and 17. Incidentally, WC does not stand for Weapons Carrier; it is simply Dodge's factory model code for 1941, following from its predecessor, the VC. Dodge changed its code every year, though not necessarily in strict alphabetical order, and the second letter referred to the vehicle size.

by the simple, tough 79bhp (60kW) 201cu in (3.3ltr) straight-six side-valve engine. Numbered by the military as the T202, variants included open and closed cab pickups, weapons carriers, the carryall steel-bodied utility, reconnaissance and radio reconnaissance cars, and closed cab trucks with either an open top or a tipper body. Some 5,000 were made at the new Mount Road, Michigan, plant. They were too early to see active service with the US armed forces.

The civilian sheet metal was found to be too fragile and complicated to repair in military service, so in 1941 it was replaced. The annual model code was WC and new military number was T215. It had simpler, if somewhat inelegant sheet metal bolted to the original civilian pattern cab, shared with the Canadian built T212 already in service with the Allies. On either a 116in (295cm) or 123in (312cm) wheelbase, power was from a slightly larger, 218cu in (3.6ltr) version of the side-valve six.

Dodge ¾-Ton

In giving a ½-ton grading to a 1-ton truck, Dodge had acknowledged that military service

was far tougher than civilian life, and the ½-ton WC's had some shortcomings. They stood high off the ground, and with the standard 60in (152cm) track, the high centre of gravity resulted in too many turning over in the inexperienced hands of drafted GI's. The tyres were too narrow to handle the soft mud found in Europe or the sands of North Africa. In 1942, the Army Ordnance Department, which in that year had taken over the task of procuring soft-skinned vehicles from the Quartermaster Corps, oversaw the replacement of the T215 with a new, reconfigured Dodge model. This was the T214, still with Dodge's WC code. The track was widened by 5in (13cm) and the wheelbase shortened, on the command car and weapons carrier, to 98in (249cm). The wheelbase of the ambulance went down from 122 to 121in (310 to 307cm), and that of the carryall was reduced by 2in to 114in (by 5cm to 290cm). The payload was upped to ¾-ton and with the squat, wide stance they looked like a military truck rather than a converted civilian model. Under the bonnet was a 230cu in (3.9ltr) 92bhp (69kW) six-cylinder engine, which would find its way into surviving T215s.

The ¼-ton WC52 weapons carrier was just one version of the Dodge T214. Note its wider track, shorter length and fatter tyres in comparison with its ½-ton predecessor. Used by British and American forces during the war, there were many other variants, including ambulances, tow trucks and command cars.

Variants of the 80,000 made included the open and closed cab WC52 weapons carriers, WC42 radio panel vans, WC17 'carryall' utilities, WC54 ambulances and WC58 command cars. A 1-ton version, the M6 gun carriage was also built. The biggest variants were the 6×6 WC63 and WC62 personnel and cargo carriers. These were brought on line as the US Army increased the size of its rifle squads from eight to twelve men and bigger trucks were required to carry them as a single unit. All would use the same engine, transmission and ancillaries, have all-wheel drive through a single-speed New Process transfer box and four-speed manual transmission and hydraulic brakes. This made maintenance in the field a much simpler operation than had been found in France in the Great War. This advantage would be something that the Army would not forego.

The Dodge, it can be seen, provided an extremely versatile base for a variety of roles from weapons carrier to ambulance to general service truck. It did a phenomenal amount of work in the Second World War, and it might be argued that it did it with considerably less glory than the jeep. The Dodge also illustrated how a commercially available vehicle could be adapted to meet military requirements, and it also showed how a base vehicle could be adapted to a variety of roles. The T214/WC Dodge might be labelled the first high mobility, multi-purpose wheeled vehicle. Because of its versatility, load capacity and off-road ability, the Dodge, rather than the jeep as has been commonly believed, could be called the grandfather of the Humvee.

Enthusiasts claim that the Dodge was the first to be given the name 'jeep', and there is evidence to support this. Before the Draft of 1940, all American soldiers were enlisted men and had, naturally, established their own way of doing things. Every new vehicle that came to the military for assessment was labelled 'Government Property' or GP, and this was corrupted to 'jeep'. When the Dodge T202 arrived it too got labelled as the new 'jeep'. When huge numbers of drafted GIs arrived they too had already heard of the new ¼-ton 'blitz buggy' vehicle being referred to as a 'jeep'. Thus the name used by the majority prevailed for the smaller newcomer and Dodge trucks were rechristened 'beep' or 'big jeep'. Too often it has been said that GP stood for 'general purpose' and a US Army publicity film from 1945

compounded the myth. The fact is that the US military never used the term 'general purpose'. The expression used was 'general *service*', so the idea that jeep was a corruption of 'general purpose' is unfounded.

ABOVE: The WC54 ¾-ton ambulance. Its main function was the transfer of troops from front-line dressing stations to hospitals.

Korea

After the Second World War the new President, Harry S Truman, severely cut defence spending and, much as they had to in the 1920s, the armed

An M1A1 White reconnaissance car. With armour and machine guns, it slotted in between the full armoured car and the Dodge weapons carrier. Much later this concept would be adopted for Humvee variants.

forces had to make do with wartime leftovers. Consequently, when the Communist invasion of South Korea pushed the new United Nations into war, the US Army's equipment was found wanting. Even if they had new vehicles, the severe climate and terrain of Korea were desperate challenges for them. Ageing wartime model jeeps were struggling in the mud, rocks and snow. An uprated Jeep, the M38, was quickly brought into service while an all-new model, the M38A1, was developed.

Greater Standardization

It was not just the jeep that was replaced by a new version. In 1949 Dodge was to supply a replacement for the T214 in the shape of the T245. At 1,000lb (454kg) heavier than the previous model, it used the old faithful 230cu in (3.8ltr) side-valve six, driving through a four-speed manual gearbox and a two-speed transfer box. It too was the base for a number of variants: the M37 utilities truck,

the M42 command post, the M43 ambulance and the M201 maintenance truck. Like its predecessor, it was a tough, simple, reliable truck. It was to last longer in service than its predecessor, with over 136,000 examples delivered to many countries around the world.

Following the Korean War the US government cut back on defence spending once more. Concentrating on nuclear weaponry, President Eisenhower looked to get 'more bang for the buck', and the Army's inventory suffered in consequence. The prolonged stand-off that was the Cold War did at least give those in charge of producing military vehicles the time to concentrate on standardization, with the aim of improving serviceability and reducing costs. The 6×6 2½-ton truck of World War II showed the way for medium/heavy truck design, and a new standardized M35 'Eager Beaver' was introduced in this category in 1950. This new truck, christened 'deuce and a half' like its forebear, had a fine turn of speed off-road, and the whine of

A preserved Dodge M37, in utility truck configuration. Its World War II heritage is clear.

RIGHT: The unsuccessful Chevrolet contender for the XM715 contract.

BELOW RIGHT: The M715 in M142 command post configuration.

A 6×6 articulated tractor-trailer unit with four-wheel steering and a 1¼-ton payload was built between the late 1960s and the mid 1970s by Consolidated Diesel Electric Company (CONDEC). Its name was derived from that of Roger Gamaunt, the designer of the articulated joint that both connected the two halves of the vehicle and transmitted the drive to the rear wheels, and 'goat' from its off-road capability.

The Goat was a short-wheelbase, four-wheeled tractor fixed in unit with a two-wheeled trailer. The components were pivoted in relation to each other in pitch and roll, but unlike conventional trailer units, not in yaw. Instead, all three driven axles remained parallel to each other in the vertical plane. The front wheels of the tractor steered in normal fashion, the centre wheels remained in the same plane and the trailer axle was mechanically steered in the opposite direction at a ratio of 50 per cent of the angle of the front wheels. The tractor unit had a rear mounted Detroit Diesel 3-53 diesel engine, putting the driver and passenger well forward in the vehicle. The open trailer could carry either cargo or troops along each side on folding seats or be fitted with an ambulance body.

The M561 body was made of aluminium and the vehicle had an amphibious capability on

If not for its olive green paint and military numbers, the M561 Gama Goat could be mistaken for a specialist industrial vehicle rather than a military one. It was too expensive, too limited in its role, too complex to maintain and too noisy and difficult to drive to be successful.

inland waters. While its performance off-road was considered good, mechanical problems made the Gama Goat unreliable in service. It was also noisy and its peculiar steering required specialist driver training. The permanent set-up of the Gama Goat also restricted its adaptability. It did not meet its service requirement adequately, and, after 11,000 vehicles were adopted for service, no more were ordered.

Wheels

The Special Analysis of Wheeled Vehicles (WHEELS) existed between February 1972 and April 1973 to study the wheeled vehicle needs of the US Army. The WHEELS committee

recommended that of the 600,000 motor vehicles then in service, standard civilian types could fulfil the work of some 400,000 of these. The first outcome was a reassessment of the 1¼-ton truck, in 4×2 and 4×4 types, from which a requirement was issued for over 33,000 new civilian-based trucks. Under the XM861/XM880 programme, four companies put forward bids: AM General, the existing supplier, Ford, Chevrolet and the previously displaced Dodge. It was Dodge's bid that secured a contract, starting in 1975, for a militarized version of its Sweptline W200 4×4 and D200 4×2 trucks. These were numbered M880 and M890, respectively, and 40,000 were supplied. The Dodge served until the beginning of this century, replacing all the M715s and M37s. Versions also included an ambulance (M886), a shelter carrier (M885) and a contract maintenance vehicle. Power was from a 318cu in (5.2ltr) petrol V8 driving through a three-speed Loadflite commercial automatic transmission and, on the 4WD M880, a New Process NP203 two-speed transfer box.

The Need for Rationalization

By the mid 1970s there were several vehicle types in service; the latest Dodge trucks, some leftover M715s, the MUTT and the Gama Goat, each performing tasks that at many points overlapped. For instance, the MUTT was used in the role of weapons carrier and ambulance. The M715 and the Dodge were shelter carriers, cargo/troop carriers, ambulances and maintenance trucks and the Gama Goat was a cargo/troop carrier, a shelter carrier and an ambulance. The M880, essentially a civilian vehicle, was not as good off-road as the oddball Gama Goat, which itself had not met all that was desired of it. The M715 was due for retirement. With this number of types in service, more spares had to be carried and thus the more there was for the mechanics to learn.

There was now a need to reappraise the situation, both from a logistic and a financial point of view. The sheer cost of developing motor vehicles had risen in real terms at a fantastic rate. Military vehicles are inherently more expensive than civilian vehicles for two reasons: first, they are produced in much smaller volumes. Chevrolet made more than 600,000 full-sized passenger cars in 1975 alone. The jeep, probably the most numerous of World War II vehicles, took four years of all-out wartime production to reach the same figure. Makers of passenger cars had at least the benefits of large volume sales where they could spread the development costs and reduce the unit price. Secondly, military vehicles need to be built to a much stronger standard than passenger cars, which further adds to the cost. The colossal inflation of the mid 1970s did nothing to help, either with the bottom-line costs or with the shape of the American economy. The Vietnam War and the ever-rising price of oil made for difficulties all round. Two pressures were placed

on the government: one was to reduce taxes, which had been raised to cover the costs of the war. The other was to cut defence spending, simply because Americans had seen too many of their young men coming home in body bags from a war that they did not see as directly jeopardizing their country's security.

The M885 Shelter Carrier version of the Dodge M880, quite plainly a militarized civilian vehicle. There lay its strength, in the low cost of its major components, and its weakness in that it was not always as strong as it needed to be for combat duty.

2 From XR311 to HMMWV – Ten Years' Gestation

Just like the Jeep, the seed that grew into the Humvee germinated as much in an auto company's research and development department as it did in the military. In 1969, two years after the Six Day War between Israel and its Arab neighbours, FMC (formerly the Food Machinery and Chemical Corporation) of San Jose, California, manufacturers of tracked military vehicles, started the development of the XR311. This was a prototype high-mobility scout car, using a tubular space frame chassis and a rear-mounted 200bhp 360cu in (5.9ltr) big-block Chrysler V8 petrol engine. It bore a strong resemblance to a 'dune buggy', a sports vehicle usually based on the Volkswagen Beetle.

But the XR311 was much bigger and tougher than a Beetle-based dune buggy. Its roots went

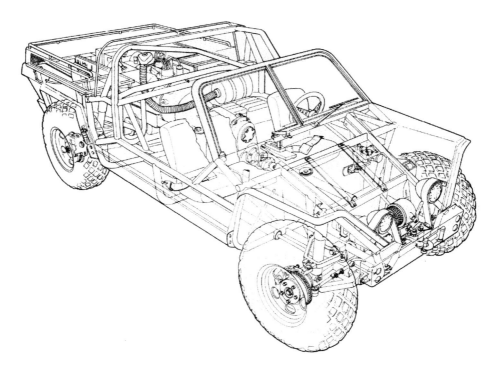

The first type XR311 in cutaway. The tubular space frame is clearly shown. The transfer box is placed between the seats. Note how the front driveshaft is offset to the bottom of the box, rather than the side as is common in so many 4WD vehicles. This is because the engine is mounted above the rear axle, putting the centreline of the crankshaft high in relation to the vehicle.

FMC XR311

Engine: First Generation

Type	Chrysler V8 liquid-cooled, petrol
Capacity	5.9ltr (360cu in)
Horsepower	180bhp (134kW) @ 4,000rpm
Compression ratio	8.4:1
Electrical system	24V

Engine: Second and Third Generation

Type	Chrysler Y8 series water-cooled OHV petrol V8
Capacity	5.2ltr (318cu in)
Bore and stroke	3.91 × 3.31in (9.93 × 8.41cm)
Compression ratio	8.6:1
Horsepower	197bhp (147kW) @ 4,000rpm
Torque	292lbft (396Nm) @ 2,200rpm
Electrical system	24V

Transmission

Gearbox	Chrysler A727 3-speed automatic
Ratios	1st: 2.45:1, 2nd: 1.45:1, 3rd: 1.00:1, reverse: 2.20:1
Transfer box	single-speed, direct drive with full-time, 4-wheel drive

Running Gear

Axles	front and rear: single-speed hypoid with no-spin feature
Axle ratios	5.98:1
Brakes	hydraulically-operated, ventilated 11.0in (28cm) discs front and rear, failsafe disc calliper parking brake on differential pinion
Suspension	4-wheel independent, double A-frame with torsion bars
Steering	power-operated with ratio variable between 16:1 and 13:1
Tyres	12.4 × 16

Construction

Chassis and bodywork	tubular steel welded, unitized body frame construction, seating 5

Dimensions

Length	175.75in (446cm)
Height	60.5in (154cm)
Width	76in (193cm)
Wheelbase	121in (307cm)
Track, front and rear	64in (162.6cm)
Ground clearance (under chassis)	14in (35.6cm)
Fuel tank capacity	30 US gal (114ltr)
Kerb weight	4,506lb (2,046kg)
Gross vehicle weight	7,200lb (3,270kg)

Performance

Maximum speed	67mph (108km/h)
Cruising range	300 miles (480km)
Angle of approach	63 degrees
Angle of departure	45 degrees
Fording depth (unprepared)	30in (76cm)
Height of centre of gravity	38.3in (97.3cm)
Turning circle	48ft (14.6m)

back to the 'Baja Boot', an extremely tough, most successful entrant of the Baja 500 off-road race down the deserts of the Baja California peninsula of Mexico. The XR311 was effectively a militarized version of the Baja Boot. Its concept was, in effect, a mixture of 'super jeep' and beach buggy, building the light arms carrying capability and off-road performance requirements of the jeep and the MUTT into a vehicle with higher off-road speed and better highway performance.

FMC offered the XR311 to the Army's Land Warfare Laboratory for evaluation. Testing the two examples presented, they liked it in principle. Ten variants, powered by 318cu in (5.2ltr) small block Chrysler V8 petrol engines, were delivered in November 1971 to the Army Armor and Engineer Board, who tested them over about 199,000 miles (320,000km) at their establishment at Fort Knox. Four examples were fitted with the Hughes-developed TOW anti-aircraft missile system, three examples were configured for unarmoured reconnaissance, and the remaining three were up-armoured for escort and security work. The last were fitted at various times with different standard issue machine guns

including a .50 Browning and the NATO standard 7.62 calibre, on different mounts. The Army liked what it found, but as with the original Bantam in the jeep's story, they did not take up the idea immediately. Defence spending would be on the decline as US troops were being pulled out of Vietnam. The American people had had enough of war.

FMC, however, were optimistic about the XR311. They developed a third-generation model for sale to 'approved users', selling several to Israel. AM General had also entered an agreement to build the vehicle under licence if it were adopted by the US Army. AM General were a wholly owned subsidiary of the American Motors Corporation, then owners of the Jeep brand name and already major military and public service vehicle contractors to the US government. And when the Army declined the XR311, FMC decided to concentrate on its tracked vehicles and sold the rights to it to AM General.

When President Carter took office in 1977 the demands made on his defence budget would be understandably lower in real terms after Vietnam, even though the high inflation of the late 1970s did little to improve the bottom line. Carter

Left open to the weather in a scrapyard, one of the XR311 prototypes submitted to the US Army's Land Warfare Laboratory. This development has a different headlight arrangement from the model shown in cutaway.

The rear-mounted engine takes up a great deal of room in the XR311.

worked hard to try to end the escalating expense of the nuclear arms race and the spectre of world annihilation that it evoked. But world events, particularly in Iran, made him change his plans regarding conventional forces. Korea and Vietnam had shown that in the modern world warfare would not be on a global scale but in the nature of more national conflicts. Thus to keep American interests served across the world and to keep Soviet influence at bay by increasing trade connections, Carter increased defence spending.

By 1967 the Ordnance Tank Automotive Command (OTAC) had become the Tank Automotive Command (TACOM), and in 1977 TACOM put forward the Army's new XM966 Combat Support Vehicle Program. This was to find a single vehicle that would perform the roles of several, a cargo/troop carrier, an armaments carrier and an ambulance. At least four companies responded: AM General, Chrysler, Teledyne Continental and Cadillac Gage.

The General Products Division of Teledyne Continental Motors Corporation submitted the Cheetah. The development of this vehicle was entrusted to Mobility Technology International, a division of the Chrysler Corporation. Based in Santa Clara, California, MTI were some way from Teledyne's base in Muskegon, Michigan. Teledyne acquired the complete rights to the Cheetah from Chrysler, but a second party was also interested in the Cheetah. It was the giant Lamborghini tractor and sports car manufacturer from Bologna, in northern Italy, who saw it also as a vehicle that might interest the Italian armed forces. They built a version that they introduced at the 1977 Geneva Motor Show.

The compact Teledyne Cheetah.

The Cheetah had a four-seat, aluminium and glass-fibre body on a tubular steel space frame. Power was from a 360cu in (5.9ltr) Chrysler V8, mounted directly over the centre line of the back axle, driving through a Chrysler A727 three-speed automatic transmission and a Full Trac full-time four-wheel-drive transfer box. Although this layout allowed more passenger room it moved the centre of gravity rearwards and higher than might be necessary, which tended to make the vehicle unstable. Testing took place in the Middle Eastern deserts and in the high altitudes of the Rocky Mountains over a period between 1977 and 1978.

Besides having an interest in the Cheetah, Chrysler's Defense Products Division entered the hunt with a vehicle of their own design, the High Mobility Truck. Christened the Saluki, Chrysler's XM966 vehicle was the most truck-like of the three, being based on commercially available, Dodge truck running gear with a big-block 360cu in (5.9ltr) petrol V8 mounted in the front of the vehicle. Its transmission was a Chrysler A727 three-speed automatic, coupled to a New Process NP203 2-speed transfer box that gave full-time four-wheel drive.

It is appropriate here to explain the difference between full- and part-time four-wheel drive.

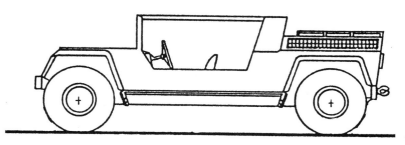

LEFT: *AM General reconfigured the XR311 as a four-seater with a vertical windscreen, as shown in this outline drawing.*

BELOW: *An outline drawing of Chrysler's ECT-based XM966 taken from their submission to TACOM.*

When a motor vehicle turns through a corner, all four wheels rotate at different speeds. The driven wheels of a two-wheel drive vehicle have a differential to allow the wheels to rotate at different speeds while still transmitting power. The other two wheels are free to rotate on the axle. In simple four-wheel-drive systems the transfer box locks the front and the rear axle together. If the vehicle is driven on a dry hard road, the difference in the rotation speed of each wheel causes a strain in the driveline, called wind-up. This may cause broken half shafts, damaged universal joints or scrubbed tyres. When the vehicle is driven off-road, the loose or soft surface allows the wheels to shrug off this wind-up with no damage. For full-time four-wheel drive to be used on the highway a centre differential had to used. New Process Gear, a Detroit-based transmission company, was one of a small number of such working on the design of a centre differential.

Others were Ferguson in England and Borg Warner in both England and the USA. Although a Ferguson transfer box, with their Duolock mechanical centre differential, was fitted to the 1966 Jensen FF sports GT (the first post-war production car to have permanent 4WD) the differential was troublesome. Only during the 1970s, as the quality of steels available improved, did the 4WD specialists begin to develop transfer boxes with centre differentials that were compact, light, reliable and at a sensible price. The heavy, bulky NP203, with its cast iron casing, had been an option on Dodge and Chevrolet light trucks since 1974. The Dodge M880 was a militarized version of a civilian truck, and the Expanded Mobility Truck would share some other common components.

But there was a more pressing reason for the EMT's commonality and conventional layout. It has to be realized that at this time Chrysler was undergoing the worst financial crisis in its history. It was in deep debt, owing money to many banks. Chrysler simply did not have the funds to develop anything of a more advanced nature.

Cadillac Gage, suppliers of wheeled armoured vehicles to the US Army, produced a prototype based on their fully armoured Commando Scout. This too used a Chrysler petrol V8. AM General based their XM966 on the XR311. The original was a two-seater, and, without increasing the overall length or the wheelbase, they reconfigured it into a four/five-seater. The windscreen was altered to one with three trapezoid, spall-resistant glasses mounted vertically so as not allow a reflection to be seen by an enemy. Each company submitted prototype vehicles in several formats, including weapons carriers, ambulances and scout vehicles. Like FMC's XR311 vehicles tested at Fort Knox, the weapons carrier variant was protected by Kevlar armour.

At one point in the XM966 programme the specifications were changed, calling for a diesel engine. Both AM General and Chrysler opted for the same engine, a 400cu in (6.6ltr) Deutz air-cooled V8, while Teledyne chose a 140hp six-cylinder Volvo diesel for the Cheetah. The programme never reached a successful conclusion, however. The US Army was widening its horizons. In 1979 it released preliminary specifications for development of a new High Mobility Multipurpose Wheeled Vehicle. This, with its practice of using initials, was presented with the rather ungainly name of the HMMWV.

What the Army now specified was a vehicle that fitted into the 1¼-ton capacity classification, but would be capable of more duties than a straightforward truck. It wanted a weapons carrier-cum-scout car like the Jeep and the MUTT, combined with a light tactical battlefield truck, an ambulance and middleweight weapons carrier for anti-aircraft guns, a troop carrier and an artillery tractor (fulfilled by the Dodge T215 and M37), plus the utility functions of the Dodge M880 and the Kaiser M715. It needed to be versatile, easily maintained, reliable and air-transportable.

These needs were clearly stated in the Program Objectives. They were to:

1. Provide a single vehicle family to satisfy joint-service requirements
2. Provide a vehicle with excellent cross-country and on-road performance
3. Provide a replacement vehicle for the M274 Mule, M561 Gama Goat and M792 ambulance

XM966 Prototypes: Teledyne Cheetah XM966

Engine (Original)
Type   Chrysler V8 liquid-cooled, petrol
Capacity   5.9ltr (360cu in)
Horsepower   180bhp (134kW) @ 4,000rpm
Compression ratio   8.4:1
Electrical system   24V

Engine (Latterly)
Type   Volvo 6-cylinder, liquid-cooled, diesel
Horsepower   140bhp (104kW)

Transmission
Gearbox   Chrysler A727 3-speed automatic
Transfer box   Full-Trac full-time, automatic 4-wheel drive, limited slip differential
                                        with variable torque distribution, chain-driven

Running Gear
Axles   front: hypoid with no-slip differential; rear: front-to-rear differential
Brakes   self-adjusting, outboard, ventilated discs on all four wheels with
                                        mechanical parking brake on rear callipers
Suspension   independent front and rear with double A arms and torsion bars,
                                        double-acting shock absorbers
Steering   variable ratio with integral hydraulic power assist

Construction
Chassis   tubular steel with integral safety cage surrounding occupants
Bodywork   4-seat aluminium with tilt-up front and rear access panels

Dimensions: Basic Model
Length   182in (462cm)
Height   65in (165cm)
Width   85in (216cm)
Wheelbase   134.4in (341.4cm)
Track, front and rear   60in (152cm)
Ground clearance   15in (38cm)

Performance
Acceleration (petrol engine)   0–30mph (0–48km/h), 5sec
Maximum speed   90mph (145km/h)
Cruising range   385 miles (620km)
Fording depth (without preparation)   36in (91cm)
Angle of approach   65 degrees
Angle of departure   46 degrees
Forward gradeability   60 per cent front
Side slope gradeability   40 per cent
Turning circle   40ft (12.2m)

XM966 Prototypes: AM General M966 Vehicle

As for the XR311, with the following changes:

Engine

Type	Deutz F8L 610 V8 air-cooled OHV diesel
Capacity	6.6ltr (400cu in)
Horsepower	160bhp (119kW) @ 3,200rpm
Torque	287lbft (389Nm) @ 2,000rpm

XM966 Prototypes: Chrysler Saluki

Engine

Type	Chrysler liquid-cooled OHV V8
Capacity	5.9ltr (360cu in)
Horsepower	195bhp (145kW) @ 4,400rpm
Torque	310lbft (420Nm)
Electrical system	12V

Transmission

Type	Chrysler A727 3-speed automatic
Transfer case	New Process 203, 2-speed with full-time 4-wheel drive

Running Gear

Axles: front	Dana 44, sprung centre section, ratio 4.88:1
Axles: rear	Dana 60 solid axle, ratio 4.88:1
Brakes: front	power-assisted disc
Brakes: rear	power-assisted drum with foot-operated parking brake on rear drums
Suspension: front	independent, double A-frame, coil springs, telescopic shock absorbers
Suspension: rear	coil springs with lower longitudinal control arms and upper triangulated control arm, telescopic shock absorbers
Steering	Saginaw 708 integral power steering unit, ratio 14:1 with Saginaw 125 pump
Tyres	4-ply, 14-18

Construction

Chassis	Dodge truck, modified ladder type
Bodywork	aluminium, 2-door with reducible height, cargo bed integral with cab

Dimensions: Basic Model

Length	176in (447cm)
Height	77in (196cm) (reducible to 60in [152cm] to top of bonnet)
Width	85in (216cm)
Wheelbase	124.4in (316cm)
Track, front and rear	70.8in (180cm)
Ground clearance	18in (46cm)
Fuel tank capacity	24 US gal (90.8ltr)

Performance

Angle of approach	63 degrees
Angle of departure	82 degrees
Height of centre of gravity	38.3in (97.3cm)
Turning circle	48ft (15m)
Range	275 miles (440km)

4. Selectively replace the M151 Jeep [*sic*] and M880 truck.

TACOM defined the roles fulfilled by the vehicles identified in objectives 3 and 4 in six categories: a forward observer vehicle, a communications vehicle, a utility truck, an ambulance, a weapon station and a personnel transport vehicle.

The specification for the HMMWV gave the requirements for the dimensions and the layout of the vehicle. Roof, bonnet height and the profile were defined and the mechanical specifications were clearly set out. Regarding objective 2, TACOM estimated that some 40 per cent of the HMMWV's time would be spent off-road, 30 per cent on the highway and 30 per cent on minor roads. But in any exercise or combat action, going from one type of terrain to another in a vehicle with part-time four-wheel drive may necessitate shifting from one drive mode to another. Shift-on-the-fly as a facility on transfer boxes was under development, so a vehicle had to stop to shift from two- to four-wheel drive – not a good idea when involved in a firefight. This was undoubtedly a reason why both Chrysler and AM General opted for full-time four-wheel drive.

The new President, Ronald Reagan, pledging to 'make America great once more', kept his election promise to rearm America. He would increase the annual defence budget from $165 billion in 1981 to $330 billion in 1987. Some of this money was spent on bringing new fighting vehicles under development into full production. These included the M1 Abrams tank and the Bradley infantry

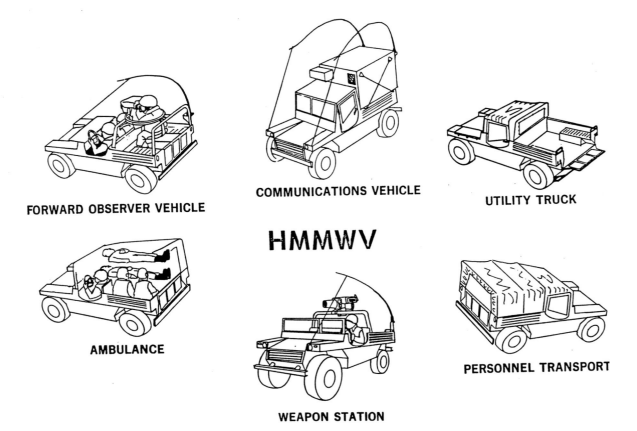

The six HMMWV variants as first envisaged by TACOM.

Looking sorry for itself in a salvage yard, a Chrysler HMMWV prototype vehicle with the lift top ambulance body. See how little ground clearance exists below the front axle.

combat vehicle. Thus the HMMWV had to have sufficient off-road capability and be fast enough to keep up with the Abrams and the Bradley in order to keep them supplied with ammunition. A further task was to ensure that the ground gained by advancing infantry units could be held by vehicle-mounted machine weapons, and supply cover from air attack. This meant that the specifications for the HMMWV were demanding. They demanded a 16in (406mm) ground clearance, the ability to climb a 60 per cent gradient, stay stable on a 40 per cent side slope, go over an 18in (457mm) vertical step and ford a depth of 30in (762mm) without prior preparation.

The specification called for a front-mounted diesel engine. Although a rear-mounted engine produced a low profile for such a big vehicle, it took up potential cargo space and created servicing difficulties in the field. This mattered little to the principles within which FMC had originally designed the XR311, a light forward observation/intercept vehicle that did not need to carry cargo as a principal requirement. The new vehicle would need, as its multipurpose tag suggested, cargo space and room for an ambulance body or a shelter.

Chrysler redesigned its XM996 vehicle, increasing the wheelbase by 10in (25.4cm), widening the track by 2in (5.5cm) and reducing the height by 5in (11cm). The air-cooled, 400cu in (6.6ltr)

Deutz F8L-610 V8 diesel motor was coupled to the same Chrysler A727 three-speed automatic gearbox. The New Process NP203 transfer box was replaced by the new NP218 transfer box. This was more compact and, with an aluminium case, much lighter. The Dana 44 True-Trac biasing differential at the front and the Dana 60 solid rear axle remained. The suspension was also the same, being independent with double A-frames and coil springs at the front with a solid axle on coil springs at the rear. The brakes were unaltered, with drums at the rear and inboard discs to the front. The conventional Dodge chassis demanded that the superstructure be above the line of the chassis, which raised the centre of gravity and thus compromised the vehicle's stability. The ground clearance was reduced to the 16in (40.6cm) required in the programme, which had the advantage of reducing the overall height. This, plus the increase in track width, helped to improve stability.

The Teledyne contender had to be redesigned totally. In doing so, the engineers produced a perimeter frame that allowed the crew to sit low in the vehicle, an arrangement that offered extra side protection. It also lowered the cargo bed, keeping the centre of gravity as low as was practicable. The six-cylinder Volvo diesel of the Cheetah was replaced by a 420cu in (6.9ltr) International Harvester V8 diesel, coupled to a General Motors 475 three-speed Turbo-Hydramatic automatic transmission, mounted in front of the new chassis. All three HMMWV contenders featured four-wheel drive as was demanded by TACOM's specification, but the Teledyne vehicle was unique in offering part-time four-wheel drive instead of the full-time system used on the other two, through the two-speed New Process NP 208 transfer box. This did not have a centre differential, which went some way to reducing the vehicle's weight and cost. Suspension was independent all round, using A-frames on variable rate longitudinal torsion bars. The aluminium body was of a four-door truck configuration, with fold-down rear seats to provide extra cargo space. Its lower profile and tapered sides were to ensure harder detection by an enemy, both visually and by radar. Engine access was by a one-piece, forward-tilting bonnet. Teledyne were highly optimistic about their chances, erecting a new factory in Seneca, California, to build the new HMMWV.

Like Teledyne, AM General had to start afresh. They had much experience from which to work, being owners of the Jeep brand name and they had made M151 MUTTS under contract. They also had an existing five ¼-ton chassis, which was one up on Teledyne. This was the M715, one of the vehicles that would be replaced by the HMMWV. The M715 was a conventional truck with a double-drop, ladder frame and semi-elliptical springs front and rear supporting live beam axles. It had a wheelbase of 126in (320cm), somewhere between the 121in (307cm) and 132in (332cm) of the two contemporary civilian Senior Jeep trucks. There was also a revised version made for sale to approved users, the AM715, which used a 132in wheelbase.

The component suppliers, including New Process Gear, had plenty of transmission options to choose from, including the new NP218

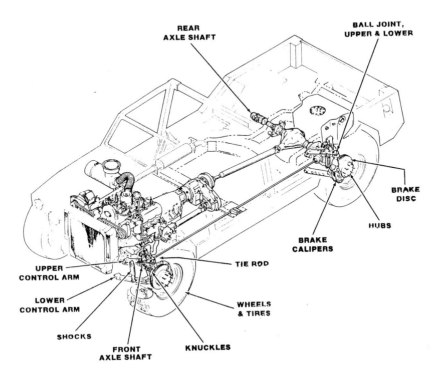

The Teledyne HMMWV contender in cutaway. The perimeter frame is visible as well as the driveline arrangement, the torsion bar suspension and the outboard brakes.

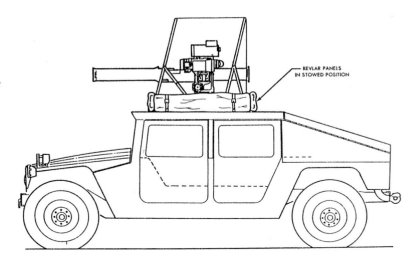

AM General's submission to the HMMWV programme in TOW missile configuration. Note the dotted line, indicating the location of the driveline within the vehicle's interior. The requirement for a Kevlar shield around the missile launcher was not followed through into production.

KEVLAR PANELS
IN STOWED POSITION

transfer box with its mechanical centre differential. In August AM General built a pilot vehicle in weapons-carrier configuration, to the provisional specification. A ladder chassis, based on that of the Senior Jeep and M715, replaced the XR311's space frame. The frame rails were like the SJ's, being a conventional double-drop design, with eight cross-members instead of the civilian model's six. The frame rails, however, were parallel and placed as close together as possible to the drivetrain to create a backbone.

In the front of the frame was a diesel engine. The first data that AM General submitted to TACOM specified the 400cu in (6.6ltr) Deutz V8 as used in the XR311, mated to a three-speed Chrysler automatic transmission with ratios identical to that used in the ECT. But shortly it was changed to a General Motors diesel of 379cu in (6.1ltr) producing 130bhp (97kw) at 3,600rpm, mated to a General Motors THM400HD Hydramatic three-speed automatic transmission. The choice of this engine was a good one; it was already in use in a number of US Army M1008 CUCV (Commercial Utility Cargo Vehicle) category vehicles, also built by General Motors. This followed the Army's principle to simplify maintenance, and in moving from gasoline to either diesel or dual-fuel engines, establishing the principle of 'one fuel at the front'.

The transfer box was also the same as on the Chrysler vehicle, a New Process NP218 full time, four-wheel-drive unit. This contained a mechanical centre differential. The suspension, front and rear, was a double A-frame arrangement with coil springs, using as many identical components as possible. The driveshafts were the same at both ends too. This was also in line with the Army's requirement to simplify maintenance. The idea of duplicating front and rear suspension and driveline components had been used in the MUTT, but in practice this compromised on-road handling and thus had not worked quite as well as had been expected. It would remain to be seen whether it worked in AM General's HMMWV pilot vehicle.

By the February of 1980 AM General had put their HMMWV through more than 17,000 miles (27,400km) of testing at their own facility. With the knowledge thus gathered, they built five vehicles that were sent to the Nevada Auto Test Center, near Carson City. The NATC is a privately owned company, a division of Hodges Transportation Inc, and provides comprehensive vehicle-testing facilities for both civilian and military vehicles, including firing ranges for weapons. The purpose of these tests, which were carried out over 50,000 miles (80,500km), was to try to reproduce as closely as possible the sort of trial the Army would give the vehicles. This would, it

TACOM

TACOM, the Tank-Automotive and Armor Command, is the organization responsible for securing all of the US Army's vehicles, armoured and soft-skinned, and for ensuring that Army personnel are trained in the correct maintenance of them. When the US Army first began buying motor vehicles in the early 1900s it was the job of the Ordnance Corps to find civilian trucks that would do the job. Considering that the automotive industry was still in its formative years, the trucks of the time served the Army well enough then, and through the Great War.

As far as tanks were concerned, the US Army built its own in 1917, but they never saw service in Europe, and in the years between the wars the Army largely disregarded tank design and development. This state of affairs was not a problem until the late 1930s, but events in Europe and Japan were to change things. As Lt Gen Brekon B. Somervell, then head of the US Army's Services of Supply, put it, 'When Hitler hitched his chariot to an internal combustion engine, he opened up a new battle front – a front that we know well. It's called Detroit.'

And it was one of Detroit's top men, William S. Knudsen, that President Roosevelt appointed to head the new National Defense Advisory Commission, with the task of getting the armed forces up to strength for a war in which the USA was not yet an active combatant. 'Big Bill' Knudsen knew all about the auto industry. It had been his job to bring Henry Ford's moving assembly line into being, a change that brought the price of a Model T tumbling between 1910 and 1917. He left Ford in 1921. The next year he joined General Motors's Chevrolet Division, rising to the post of president of the whole Corporation by 1937.

Danish-born Knudsen knew how to make cars, he knew the strengths and the weakness of the automobile companies, and, most importantly, he knew its people. When drafted into the Army to head the NDAC, he showed no favouritism for his old employers when he asked Chrysler's president, Kaufmann T. Keller, to build him some tanks. In its sixteen-year history Chrysler had established a reputation for engineering quality, but their resources would be put to the test. Keller, it was said, responded to Knudsen's request by agreeing, and then asked where he could see a tank. Chrysler's engineers began by building a wooden mock-up of the Army's current model, the M2A1, in the Dodge plant in Rock Island, Illinois, but the Corporation did not have space in any of its existing plants to meet the NDAC's demands. By the autumn of 1940, more than a year before America entered the war, the government provided $21 million for a completely new factory. Built in Warren township, north of Detroit, the huge plant was named the Detroit Arsenal, and between Easter 1941 and May 1945 the workers there turned out over 22,000 tanks.

But all this industry needed organization. The auto manufacturers, all geared to the war effort, needed to know how many vehicles to make, to what design, how many spare parts to make and where to send their products. The US Army's head of Ordnance, Lt Gen Levin H. Campbell went to Detroit in 1942 to set up the Tank-Automotive Center. It was another drafted GM executive, ex-Pontiac man Brig Gen Alfred Glancy who was to lead the new organization, soon to be renamed 'Office, Chief of Ordnance-Detroit' (OCO-D), and would be responsible for procuring and delivering all the Allied armed forces' land vehicles that were of US manufacture. Most importantly, it was the OCO-D that made the Army realize how important industry's contribution was in providing the best equipment.

The OCO-D was, however, broken up in 1945. Chrysler lost control of the Detroit Arsenal and OCO-D's duties were transferred there. At the outbreak of the Korean War, when the Army was still using many World War II vehicles, OCO-D's duties were taken over by the new Ordnance Tank-Automotive Center (OTAC). The Detroit Arsenal was given back to Chrysler, who continued to make M47 tanks there. The Cold War ensured that the Army and industry would continue to co-operate on development and manufacture of military hardware. As indicated in the main text, by 1967 OTAC was known as the Tank Automotive Command (TACOM), based at the Detroit Arsenal at Warren, and would work with contractors in the private sector to procure the kind of vehicle that would best suit the Army's needs.

The Vietnam War proved the worth of the alliance between TACOM and industry, as the Detroit Arsenal made M60 Patton tanks and M113 APCs. Born out of the experience gained in the Yom Kippur war, which emphasized the need for fast, highly mobile armour, the M1 Abrams is perhaps the finest battle tank yet made. It was introduced in 1982 and was the most effective destroyer of Iraqi armour in the Gulf War. A year after the M1's introduction, Chrysler sold its Defense Products Division to General Dynamics.

In the 1990s TACOM's acronym remained the same but the meaning was expanded to the Tank-Automotive and Armaments Command as its role grew to take over control of the arsenals at Rock Island, Illinois and Picatinny, New Jersey and the maintenance depots at Texarkana, Texas and Anniston, Alabama. TACOM's role was spreading also into the total logistical support for US forces across the world, through its Local Area Representatives (LARs).

As the nature of war has changed, so has the role of the Army. Nowadays the importance of anti-terrorist campaigns, peacekeeping and humanitarian missions following natural and man-made disasters is now as prominent, if not more so, than outright face-to-face conflict. The world's armies need to be light, quickly deployable and highly flexible, and fighting vehicles need to be lighter, tougher and more reliable. TACOM's subsidiary, the Tank Automotive Research Development and Engineering Center, has the task of predicting the US armed forces' needs for the future and of developing the vehicles and logistics support they will need.

(The author is indebted to Ann M. Bos, Command Historian and Randy R. Talbot, Historian, TACOM for their help.)

was hoped, minimize the failure rate and demonstrate that this was the best vehicle they could put forward to win the contract.

By February 1981 TACOM had finalized the specifications for the HMMWV programme, coded XM998, and sent out invitations to sixty-one manufacturers. Out of five organizations that submitted proposals to TACOM by the following April, three were given the opportunity to present prototypes for testing. They were: Teledyne Continental Motors, who bid $3.5 million, Chrysler Corporation who tendered a bid of $4.1 million, and AM General, whose bid was for $4 million. Each would have to deliver eleven prototypes for testing by May 1982.

The Major Performance Requirements were:

Gross vehicle weight	7,200lb (3,268kg)
Payload	2,500lb (1,135kg)
Range	300 miles (483km)
Maximum speed	60+mph (97+km/h)
Acceleration (0–30mph [48km/h])	6–8sec
Ballistic protection	16g fragment @ 225m/s
Engine	diesel
Transmission	automatic

The principal dimensions would be:

Maximum width	85in (216cm)
Maximum length	195in (495cm)
Height (reducible)	69in (175cm)

The dimensions, along with the gross vehicle weight, would ensure that the HMMWV could be transportable in a range of aircraft then in service with the US Air Force's Air Mobility Command. These, for strategic deployment, were the fixed-wing Lockheed C-130 Hercules, the Lockheed C141 Starlifter and the Lockheed C5A Galaxy. For tactical deployment, the new vehicle would also need to be transportable by helicopter: the Sikorsky UH-60 Black Hawk, the Boeing CH-47 Chinook and the Sikorsky CH-53E Super Stallion.

This was a race AM General could not afford to lose. Pride and heritage were at stake as well as money. AM General's parent company, the American Motors Corporation were owners of the Jeep brand name and had a long heritage of making military vehicles, but AMC were in deep financial trouble. Their non-automotive operations helped keep them afloat, but 1979 was the only year in that decade where the automotive division showed a profit, thanks to the fact that for the first time ever it made more Jeeps, which sold well, than passenger cars, which didn't. In 1979 AMC had signed a letter of intent with the French manufacturer Renault to build Renault passenger cars in the USA. The Renault connection would come too late to affect the financial troubles in which AMC were to find themselves in 1980. A fuel crisis had hit America and Americans demanded the small-engined, fuel-efficient compact cars. AMC had compact cars but not small engines. Even Jeeps, with their big six-cylinder and V8 motors, were rejected by the public. In 1981 it was announced that Renault would be designing all AMC's new passenger cars. These European-type cars with European appetites for fuel were AMC's best hope to return to profit. The change would also have repercussions for AM General.

3   The Pre-Production Tests

Each manufacturer involved in the HMMWV programme was required to supply eleven prototypes for testing. Each would be fitted out as a cargo/troop carrier, a TOW missile carrier, an armament carrier, a shelter carrier and an ambulance. The US armed forces had a number of testing grounds around the USA that provided a variety of climates. They chose several to evaluate the prototypes. AM General's eleven vehicles were constructed, in addition to the five that were being tested at the National Automotive Test Center.

Each manufacturer had his own interpretation of how some of these variants should be built. There were to be three different ambulance variants, a soft-top, a mini and a maxi. Both General Dynamics and Teledyne used a mini ambulance body with a roof that could be raised, to be easily

transportable, but still give adequate capacity. This would enable the variant to be carried in the CH53 and the CH47 helicopter.

The pre-production models underwent Phase I, the Durability and Operational Testing (DT/OT). Commencing on 1 July 1982, these tests would assess the prototypes in two contrasting climates.

The Army used Aberdeen, Maryland for European-type environmental tests, and Yuma, Arizona for desert conditions. In both venues trained vehicle testers and engineers would find out whether the prototypes were tough enough to stand up to combat, and, secondly, to see how easily the Humvee could be maintained in the field. The Army's requirements were neatly encapsulated in the self-explanatory phrase 'Mean Miles Between Mission Failure' (MMBMF). The tests were for

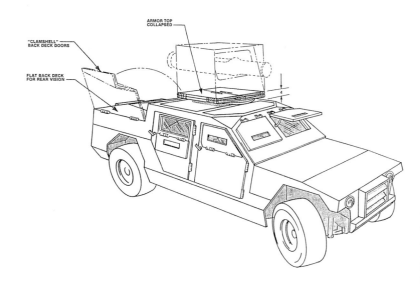

The Teledyne Continental TOW Missile variant, showing the positions of the operator and loader. The demountable Kevlar panels to protect the operator are shown here in outline. This feature would not be carried forward to the production vehicles.

performance – acceleration and fuel consumption, etc. – for the ease with which they could be loaded into aircraft, and for off-loading from low-altitude aircraft using the LAPES (Low Altitude Parachute Extraction System). There were also exhaustive tests with the TOW missile system, the .50in and the 7.62 calibre machine gun and the 40mm grenade launcher fitted to the weapons carrier versions. Teledyne's weapons carrier was configured to mount the TOW missile, the M60 7.62 and the M2 .50in machine gun and the Mk19 40mm automatic grenade launcher. AM General's eleven vehicles encountered problems with the brakes, the fuel system and the power steering, and the designers then had to make appropriate modifications before Phase II.

AM General's XM998 HMMWV Prototype

Engine: Original Submission

Type	General Motors V8 diesel, liquid-cooled
Capacity	6.1ltr (372cu in)
Horsepower	130bhp (97kW) @ 3,600rpm
Torque	260lbft (353Nm) @ 2000rpm

Engine: Pre-Production Version

Type	General Motors V8 diesel, liquid-cooled
Capacity	6.2ltr (378cu in)
Bore and stroke	100 × 97mm (3.98 × 3.82in)
Compression ratio	21.5:1
Horsepower	150bhp (120kW) @ 3,600rpm
Torque	260lbft (353Nm) @ 2000rpm

Transmission

Gearbox	Chrysler A727 3-speed automatic
Transfer box	New Process NP218 218 2-speed with full-time, 4-wheel drive

Running Gear

Axles	AMC/Jeep front and rear in suspended carrier
Axle ratios	4.56:1
Brakes, front and rear	Kelsey Hayes AMG 66 power-assisted disc, inboard, mounted on the differential
Suspension, front and rear	independent, double A-frame, coil springs, front stabilizer bar, telescopic shock absorbers
Steering	Saginaw 708 integral power steering unit, ratio variable between 13:1 and 16:1, Saginaw 125 pump
Wheels	steel disc, 8-bolt
Tyres	4–36 × 12.5-16.5LT, with Goodyear 2-piece aluminium insert

Construction

Chassis	boxed double drop with ladder-type cross-members
Bodywork	aluminium, 4-door, bonded and riveted

Dimensions: Basic Model

Length	185in (470cm)
Wheelbase	130in (330cm)
Track, front and rear	71.6in (182cm)
Ground clearance	16in (40.6cm)
Total fuel tank capacity	25 US gal (94.6ltr)

AM General

Nash and Hudson
AM General's history goes back to the very early days of the American auto industry, and includes such famous but now defunct names as Rambler, Studebaker, Willys-Overland and Kaiser. Thomas Jeffery made the Rambler bicycle in Conch, Wisconsin, and in 1902, like so many of his contemporaries, turned to automobile manufacture. He named his successful little car the Rambler after the bicycle. In 1911 he added trucks to his product line, including the four-wheel-drive, four-wheel-steer Quad. Jeffery was on board the liner *Lusitania* in 1915 when it was torpedoed. He survived, and the following year sold his company, along with the Kenosha, Wisconsin factory, to the former General Motors executive Charles Nash.

Nash was as good a production man as he was a financial expert, and his conventional, economical, well-made cars made Nash a profitable company. The post-World War II cars were, like almost all other makers' offerings, revamps of pre-war models. However, the new 1949 models were quite different, with a 'streamlined' appearance. Nash took a different route, too, with the introduction of the compact Rambler. It was the only serious domestic entrant in this sector of the market, taking over from Willys-Overland.

Against competition from the 'Big Three' of General Motors, Ford and Chrysler, the 'independent' makers would be fighting a battle that they would ultimately lose. Amalgamation seemed to be the most obvious answer for success. In 1954 Nash joined forces with the equally hard-pressed Hudson to form the American Motors Corporation. The Hudson was also an old make, started in 1909 by Roy D. Chapin and named after Hudson's department store in New York which provided the start-up capital. Hudson's story is not unlike Nash's: conventional cars that sold well in the 1920s and the 1930s but which went out of favour in the post-war years when neither could offer a V8 engine.

Kaiser-Frazer
One maker that did not start post-war production with pre-war models, because it was a newcomer, was Kaiser-Frazer. The millionaire industrialist Henry J. Kaiser got together with the ex-Willys-Overland vice-president Joseph Frazer in 1941 to plan a new peacetime auto-making venture. In Ford's Willow Run wartime bomber factory they produced two modern looking cars: the Kaiser and the more expensive Frazer. Although they sold well in the early post-war years, they lost out as the biggest companies got their new models into the showrooms. Kaiser-Frazer's problems were twofold: their cars were expensive and the company could not afford to produce the V8 engine they had under development. Sales plummeted. Buyers also stayed away, in large measure because they thought the company had no future. Kaiser needed a partner with some history, and that partner was Willys-Overland.

Willys-Overland
John North Willys was a natural salesman. At the end of the nineteenth century in his hometown of Canandaigua, New York, he sold bicycles and, from 1901 on, automobiles, including the Rambler and the Overland. When the latter company failed to deliver, he took it over. His acumen pushed the new Willys-Overland to second place in US sales behind Ford. The year 1926 saw the introduction of the Whippet, an economical, lightweight car with a four-cylinder side-valve engine. Willys's relationship with his company was a rather on-off affair. He left to pursue a diplomatic career, only to return to save the company from collapse. He recruited the lawyer George Ritter to set the company's finances straight, but Willys died suddenly in 1935 and would not see the company's most famous product, the jeep, even begin its development. His place was taken by Ward Canaday, who, with Ritter's help, restructured Willys-Overland and wiped out its debts.

The World War II jeep programme earned Willys the rights to build it in civilian form after the war. Willys also re-entered the compact car market with the new Aero, but could not produce it at anywhere near the bargain-basement price that the Whippet and its successor the American had sold for, and they found themselves in financial difficulties. Amalgamation with Kaiser, with whom they had been co-operating, was a natural move.

Under Kaiser, passenger car production was moved to new factories in Brazil and Argentina, and the Jeep brand was developed under the new company Willys Motors Inc. This was restructured as Kaiser-Jeep in 1963, and the following year Kaiser bought part of the crippled Studebaker concern.

Studebaker

The five Studebaker brothers were wagon builders who started business in 1852 in South Bend, Indiana. Car production began in 1902 with an electric vehicle and a petrol-engined car followed two years later. Truck production began in 1905 and both grew steadily. Growth was interrupted by a collapse during the 1929 Stock Market crash, but poor management delayed recovery until 1934. Wartime production included the M29 Weasel tracked vehicle and 200,000 2½-ton, 6×4 and 6×6 trucks, mostly for Allied use under Lend-Lease. The Soviet Union was the biggest recipient of the trucks, and it is said that they were so reliable that the word 'Studebaker' became the Russian soldier's expression for 'good'.

Truck production was not Studebaker's only contribution to the war effort. The company's premises were based on several sites around South Bend, but a new government-financed plant was built at the end of Chippewa Avenue close to the Pennsylvania Railroad for Studebaker to build Curtiss-Wright Cyclone aero engines. After the war, Curtiss-Wright acquired the plant, but, when demand for the Cyclone diminished, Studebaker bought the plant back and used it to build military vehicles. However, Studebaker's car business was in terminal trouble, and in 1964, after moving passenger car production to Canada, they gave up the automobile business altogether.

Kaiser were suppliers of automotive products to the US government, building M38A1 military Jeeps and DJ-5A postal Jeeps, and they were looking to expand. In 1964 they bought the Chippewa plant from Studebaker and along with it some lucrative contracts for army trucks. The new business was named the Government and Defense Product Division. But Kaiser's non-automotive concerns needed new finance, and the chairman Edgar Kaiser looked to the American Motors Corporation to raise it. Kaiser had financial interests in AMC and in December 1969 AMC bought Kaiser-Jeep. In 1971 they split the Jeep concern into two parts: the Jeep Corporation, based in Toledo, Ohio, which would make civilian Jeeps and AM General, centred in the Chippewa Plant, which would make military vehicles, postal vehicles and school buses.

While AM General's HMMWV was making progress in its DT/OT testing, the parent company, the American Motors Corporation, was undergoing the most serious crisis in its history. Under its CEO Cruse Moss, AM General was viable. In 1977 it had won an order for up to 75,000 heavy-duty military trucks, worth $252.7 million, and it was still supplying DJ-5 Jeeps for the national postal service and building transit buses. Renault had already acquired 22 per cent of AMC stock in 1979, but in order to fund the installation of new plant in AMC's factories to build Renault cars, Gerry Myers, AMC's chief executive, was forced to sell more stock to Renault. The purchase, costing the French company $122.5 million, raised their holding to 46.4 per cent. This compromised AMC, because the French government owned Renault. It would not be appropriate for an American company part-owned by a foreign government, regardless of whether it was a NATO member or not, to be building vehicles for the American armed forces. Political considerations notwithstanding, the Hummer contract would come too late to be a lifesaver for American Motors. In 1982 they were obliged to sell off AM General to the LTV Aerospace and Defense conglomerate for $170 million, a fraction of the worth of the HMMWV contract that AM General were hoping to secure.

A Painful Decision for Chrysler

It was not just AMC that were in difficulty. In the mid 1970s the Chrysler Corporation had badly lost its way. The management structure had fallen apart and, despite the integrity of the engineering department which enjoyed an enviable reputation, the cars being made were of extremely poor quality. One telling example of this was the fact that the design engineers were not conferring with the production engineers, resulting in cars that could not be built without serious re-engineering on the shop floor. Losses were mounting. The sacking of Lee Iacocca from the Ford Motor Company by Henry Ford II was Chrysler's gain. Iacocca was recruited in 1979 and began to turn the Corporation around.

The restructuring of the debt programme was backed by hard-won government guarantees. This had been achieved around 1979–80, but in the early 1980s the whole of the USA was hit by recession. High interest rates and a rise in fuel prices hit auto sales very hard. Although Iacocca had reorganized Chrysler's finances and had a new, profitable and highly saleable compact passenger car, rapidly rising interest rates on all the loans he had negotiated were harming profit margins. To keep the Corporation's head above water, and, equally important, to continue to pay his suppliers, Iacocca had to raise some cash and to do it he had to make a painful decision. He had to decide what his core business would be: cars or military vehicles. In his autobiography *Iacocca* (Lee Iacocca with William Novak, Sidgwick & Jackson, 1984) he says that he was tempted to sell the car-making operation and keep the tanks, as they virtually guaranteed a \$50million annual profit.

Not only that but he cited the engineering and management people in the Defense Products Division as some of the best in the entire Corporation. But the selling of the Defense Products Division, rather than the core auto-making business, would ensure that as many people as possible would keep their job. So for Chrysler it had to be cars, not tanks, and in 1982 the Defense Products Division was sold to General Dynamics Land Systems for \$348 million. Along with it went not only the rights to the Expanded Mobility Truck (EMT) and a place in the HMMWV programme, but the whole of the new M1 Abrams tank.

A slightly retouched picture of the General Dynamics' ECV, highlighting the windscreen and door. Compared with the Chrysler version submitted in the XM966 Program, the wheelbase is longer and the track wider. General Dynamics also reshaped the cowl and reprofiled the bonnet, giving the effect of a raised section. This no doubt improved the forward visibility while still accommodating the Deutz diesel V8. Note also the cowl of the air cleaner, not featured on Chrysler's vehicle (see page 35). This is the weapons carrier variant, but unlike the AM General or the Teledyne vehicle, it has only two doors.

Chrysler Defense Systems' (Later General Dynamics') XM998 HMMWV Prototype

Engine
Type   Deutz F8L 610 air-cooled, OHV V8 diesel
Capacity   6.56ltr (400cu in)
Bore and stroke   4 × 3.9in (102 × 100mm)
Horsepower   160bhp (119kW) @ 3,200rpm
Torque   287lbft (389Nm) @ 2,000rpm
Electrical system   24V

Transmission
Gearbox   Chrysler A727 3-speed automatic
Ratios   1st: 2.45:1, 2nd: 1.45:1, 3rd: 1.00:1, reverse: 2.20:1
Torque converter stall ratio 1.94
Transfer box   New Process NP218, 2-speed with full-time four-wheel drive
Ratios   high: 1.00:1, low: 2.61:1

Running Gear
Axles   front: Dana 44 IFS; rear: Dana 60 solid axle
Axle ratios   4.56:1
Brakes   front: power-assisted disc; rear: Bendix BX Duo-Servo drum, power-assisted with foot-operated parking brake on rear drums
Suspension   front: independent, double A-frame, coil springs, telescopic shock absorbers; rear: coil springs with lower longitudinal control arms and upper triangulated control arm, telescopic shock absorbers
Steering   Saginaw 708 integral power steering unit, ratio 14:1 with Saginaw 125 pump
Wheels   steel disc, 8-bolt
Tyres   4-ply, 37-12.5-13 LT, Patcell 'Safety Roller' run-flat

Construction
Chassis   Dodge truck, modified ladder-type
Bodywork   aluminium, 2-door with reducible height, cargo bed integral with cab

Dimensions: Basic Model
Length   188.9in (479.8cm)
Height   72.8in (184.9cm) (reducible to 58.5in [148.6cm] to top of bonnet)
Width   85in (215.9cm)
Wheelbase   134.4in (341.4cm)
Track, front and rear   72in (183.6cm)
Ground clearance   16.5in (41.9cm)
Fuel tank capacity   24 US gal (90.8ltr)

Performance
Angle of approach   60 degrees
Angle of departure   46 degrees
Height of centre of gravity 38.3in (97.3cm)
Turning circle   46.8ft (14.3m)

It is something of an irony that Chrysler, once so prominent in the defence industry with its Dodge Division and stewardship of the Detroit Arsenal, should sell off the Defense Products Division, and that American Motors should sell AM General in the same year. Only five years on, in 1987, Chrysler bought American Motors and, if AMC had held on to AM General, Chrysler

---

Teledyne Continental Motors' HMMWV Prototype

Engine
Type	International Harvester V8 liquid-cooled diesel
Capacity	6.9ltr (420cu in)
Bore and stroke	4 × 4.2in (101.6 × 106.2mm)
Horsepower	170bhp (127kW) @ 3,300rpm
Torque	310lbft (420Nm) @ 2000rpm
Electrical system	24V

Transmission
Gearbox	General Motors 475 THM 3-speed automatic
Ratios	1st: 2.48:1, 2nd: 1.48:1, 3rd: 1.00:1, reverse: 2.10:1
Transfer box	New Process 208, 2-speed, part-time, 4-wheel drive with chain drive
Ratios	high, 1:1, low, 2.6:1

Running Gear
Axles	front: Tractech True Trac with Dana model 44-IC automatic torque biasing; rear: Tractech No-Spin with Dana model 60-C automatic torque locking differential
Differential ratios	front: 4.89:1; rear: 4.88:1
Brakes	Dayton-Walther dual piston, sliding calliper ventilated discs front and rear, parking brake on rear
Suspension, front and rear	independent, double A-arms, torsion bars
Steering	Saginaw 708 integral power steering unit
Wheels	Motor Wheel 2-piece with run-flat assembly
Tyres	36 × 12.5-16.5 tubeless light truck type

Construction
Chassis	welded steel box frame with rails to protect crew
Bodywork	all-aluminium, 2/4 door with reducible height

Dimensions: Basic Model
Length	177in (449.6cm)
Height	62in (157.5cm) to top of windscreen
Width	80in (203.2cm)
Wheelbase	124in (315cm)
Track, front and rear	66in (167.6cm)
Ground clearance	14in (35.6cm)
Fuel tank capacity	30 US gal (114ltr)

Performance
Maximum speed	72mph (116km/h)
Cruising range	300 miles (483km)
Acceleration	0–30mph (0–48km/h), 6sec
Maximum grade	60 per cent fore and aft
Turning circle	50ft (15.3m)

5 The First Production Variants

The five original variants that were tested as prototypes, the cargo/troop carrier, armament carrier, TOW carrier, shelter carrier and ambulance were adopted by the US military as basic types. Using the same running gear, they were evolved into fifteen configurations for service in the US Army, the Navy, the Air Force and the Marine Corps. It will be seen that in three of the five main groups a different number has been given to an otherwise identical vehicle simply because it is fitted with a winch.

M998/M1038 Cargo/Troop Carrier

This is the basic Humvee, the Army's family station wagon, freight hauler, minibus and pick-up truck rolled into one. Its primary use is the transportation of equipment, materials and personnel. Of the two number designations, the second, M1038, simply identifies the vehicle as being fitted with a winch, the grade of which permits the recovery of similar vehicles as well as the self-recovery function.

A basic Humvee in two-door, troop carrier configuration, on duty with SFOR.

The basic skeletal body of the Humvee was designed to carry a great variety of different body configurations, and in the 'mix-and-match' M998/M1038 this may be seen most clearly. To use an old-fashioned civilian term, the cargo carrier is a roadster pick-up truck, with seating in the front for the driver and one crew member. In the two-man crew version the rear door apertures are blanked off with easily removable plates should a different configuration be required. A four-man crew version – a 'crew cab', to use another civilian term – can also be made, fitting rear doors and forward-facing passenger seats behind the driver and the front passenger. The cargo bed is thus shorter, with a reduced carrying capacity. For troop transport, longitudinal, unpadded, wooden, slatted seats are fitted in the pick-up bed over the wheel apertures. In the two-man crew version the seats provide accommodation for eight passengers, and in the four-man crew version, four passengers. The M998/M1038 can be fitted with infantry weapons, namely, a mortar and/or cannon.

The doors are of a full height, metal frame construction covered in a plastic fabric containing transparent window apertures. Like the blanking plates for the door apertures, they are easily removable. The cab roof in all cargo/troop carrier variants is also plastic fabric, as is the high tilt, which can be fitted over the pick-up bed of the two-seat configuration. The M998/M1098 has no armour of any kind fitted.

A winterization kit is available for the M998/M1038. This consists of a hard rear panel with a door and a hard front panel. The plastic fabric high tilt is fixed to this, providing a fully enclosed area. A heater can supply a controllable mixture of recirculated or fresh air to the troop/cargo enclosure through a variable-speed fan. A dome light illuminates the interior, with a blackout light providing blue light illumination during blackout conditions.

Because the M998 and M1038 both have a soft top, the windscreen may be folded down. The windscreen glass can be removed from many military vehicles, including the Humvee. This is done in bright sunshine to prevent reflections from giving away a unit's position. As another form of protection against observation, the Humvee's bonnet can be raised to shield the windscreen from the sun when parked.

M1038 cargo carrier with winch, set up as a four-door soft top. Note the extended front bumper on the M1038, concealing the winch.

ABOVE: An M998 with the high top erected. The bonnet is left open when the vehicle is parked to shield against the sun's reflection, which can give away the unit's location.

An M1045 TOW missile carrier of the US Marine Corps drives down a road in Saudi Arabia during Operation Desert Shield.

The performance of all the variants is considered to be the same, except that the winch of the M1038 variants, which protrudes from the front of the vehicle, reduces the angle of approach slightly. The M998/M1038 has a payload, including crew, of 2,500lb (1,135kg) and a gross vehicle weight (GVW) of 7,700lb (3,496kg). When driven on hard roads at an average speed of 30–40mph (48–64km/h) and using bias-ply tyres, the vehicle has a cruising range of 337 miles (543km).

The M966/M1036, M1045/M1046: TOW Missile Carrier

This is the Humvee in a specialist weapons-carrier form. The variants are numbered in a similar way to the cargo/troop carrier: the M966 does not have a winch, the M1036 does. The M966/M1036 offers some basic protection to the crew, although the vehicles are not bullet-proof. There is a hard roof and the doors, which have a

The TOW Missile

'TOW' stands for 'Tube-launched, Optically-sighted, Wire-guided'. The TOW anti-tank missile was developed by the Hughes Missile Systems Company for use by infantry. Work on the design started in 1962 with the first test-firings taking place in 1968. It entered service with the US military in 1970 and was first used in action in Vietnam in 1972, fitted to Bell UH-BB Huey helicopters. Its makers, Raytheon Systems of Arizona, have it still in production thirty years later. The TOW system has also been widely exported to users such as Bahrain, Belgium, China and Israel. In the Yom Kippur War of 1973 Israeli armed forces used it to great effect against the Soviet-supplied armour of Egypt.

A spectacular picture of a TOW missile at the point of launch. It can be seen here how the slant-back body was specifically designed to prevent damage by the missile's exhaust to the vehicle's body.

TOW Operation

The reasons for the TOW missile's popularity and longevity are the ease with which the crews can be trained to use it, its ease of transportation and simplicity of use. The missile system can be fairly quickly set up, its firepower is effective and the whole system is relatively cheap. In infantry use the glass-fibre and laminate launch tube is mounted on a tripod. The operator finds the target by using an optical sight. He launches the missile from a tube, and, as it flies, it spools out a wire. As long as the operator keeps the target in the cross-sights the missile will home in on its target. The HEAT (High Explosive Anti-Tank) warhead on the solid-fuelled missile can destroy a tank at distances of up to 4,100yd (3,750m). The two-stage BLAAM (Bunkers Light Armor and Masonry) warhead can destroy a concrete bunker.

On the M966/M1036 the TOW Missile launch tube has its own mount with a battery-operated guidance system stored in the vehicle. When installed on the Humvee, the launcher's elevation is limited to 20 degrees and its depression to 10 degrees to prevent damage to the vehicle. The cargo shell door pivots at either end. When the door forward latch is released from inside the vehicle, the door opens rearward to function as a loader's door, facilitating the mounting of the TOW launcher and missile loading. When the door rear latch is released, the door opens like a car boot or hatchback to give access to the cargo area from the rear of the vehicle. This is to allow the stowing of the TOW launcher and equipment or the operating of the TOW launcher from a mounting on the ground.

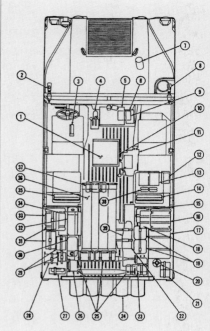

TOW missile carrier: storage and equipment load plan of the original version. Although the ammunition differs, the other armaments-carrier variants are as well laden as this.

Key:

1	Missile guidance set (MGS)		21	Combat rations
2	M16A1/M203 rifle		22	Optical sight w/cover
3	Flashlight		23	Night sight battery (under tanker roll)
4	Binoculars			
5	AN/GRC-160 radio		24	Camouflage screen and support system
6	TSEC/KY-57			
7	Gasoline cook stove (strapped to air lift bracket)		25	Tanker rolls
			26	Tripod
8	M16A1/M203 rifle		27	Telephone
9	Night sight vehicle power conditioner		28	DR8 cable reel
			29	Combat rations
10	Adjustable gunner's platform		30	M13 decontamination kit
11	Traversing unit		31	Ammunition (M16A1)
12	Radiac meter		32	Water can
13	Night vision goggles (2)		33	NBC overgarments (strapped to body)
14	NBC footwear			
15	Battery pack, night sight		34	MGS battery assemblies (2)
16	NBC overgarments (strapped to body)		35	NBC footwear (2)
			36	Missiles (6)
17	Boresight collimator		37	Tanker roll (strapped to roof)
18	Night vision sight case		38	NBC hood masks (4)
19	Coolant cartridge cases		39	Launch tube (strapped to door)
20	Radio antenna (on cargo shell)			

The 'slant-back' shape of the Humvee weapons carrier variants was not adopted for transportation or cosmetic reasons; although it gives the vehicle a well-proportioned appearance, it also reduces the carrying capacity. Its design was due to the adoption of the TOW missile. As the missile fires, the exhaust from the back of the launch tube, especially when the tube is elevated, would scorch the paint of a square-backed vehicle but not that of a slant-back. For the sake of commonality, the slant-back was universally fitted to all weapons carrier types.

distinctive cross-pattern on the outer surface, are fibreglass, reinforced with a Kevlar composite. The polycarbonate windows rise and fall. These and the windscreen are resistant to shrapnel and other debris (spall). They may resist a spent cartridge but not one fired within the range of the weapon that fired it. Damage to the engine by spall is minimized by baffles in the bonnet louvres. Run-flat tyres are fitted should any be punctured. There is also a version for the Marine Corps with Hi-hard steel plates placed over the door panels to improve resistance to fragmentation. The windows and the windscreen are 2in (56mm) polycarbonate. The doors are visually identified by a flat outer surface. It is important to recognize that the armour fitted to these variants is not proof against close-quarter fire; it will resist a spent bullet, but not one within lethal range. These up-armoured models are numbered M1045 (winch) and M1046 (without winch).

Mounting the TOW missile launcher on the roof of each missile carrier gives a 360 degree field of fire. This is limited to 300 degrees left and right when vehicle power conditioner (VPC) cables are connected. The crew use a hatch in the roof through which they can operate the weapon. Six missiles are stored in the rear compartment, which is covered by a composite hatch. Slant-backed, it is hinged at the rear and the forward edge. Thus it will open like the hatchback of a family car, allowing loading from the ground. When the crew of the vehicle go into action, the hatch can be hinged from the rear, allowing access to the weapons from the firing position.

This means that the crew do not need to dismount from the firing station to get a new missile. Although it may reduce the load space, the slant-back design has a purpose. Before a TOW missile is fired, the crew close the hatch. The slope of the hatch allows the blast from the missile to discharge without causing any damage to the vehicle's rear. The GVW of the basic M966/M1036 versions is 8,200lb (3,723kg), while the armour of the M1045/M1046 puts the weight up to 8,400lb (3,814kg). Use of the M1036 is exclusive to the US Marine Corps. The extra weight of the vehicles reduces the cruising range on hard roads to 320 miles (515km) for the M966/M1036 and 312 miles (502km) for the up-armoured variants.

The M1025/M1026 and M1043/M1044: Armament Carrier

These versions are almost identical to the M966/M1036 TOW Carrier, differing only in the type of armament carried and the mounts provided. Again, the numbering is determined by whether or not a winch is carried: M1025 if it does not, M1026 if it does. A pintle mount is fitted to the weapons ring, which can accommodate a 40mm Mk19 Mod 3 grenade launcher, an M2HB .50-calibre machine gun, an M240 7.62mm machine gun or an M60 7.62mm machine gun. The GVW is the same as for the M966/M1036. There are up-armoured versions of this variant too: the M1043/M1044. These have the same level of protection as the M966/M1036 TOW carriers, and the GVW is again the same. The cruising range for all these is the same as for the equivalent TOW missile variants.

The US Marine Corps use an exclusive up-armoured version of the M1025/M1026. It is the M1043/M1044 (non-winch and winch, respectively) which has similar armour to the M1045/M1046 with equivalent protection. The GVW is 8,400lb (3,814kg).

An M1026 armaments carrier with winch, belonging to the USAFE. Note the distinctive cross-shaped mouldings on the Kevlar-reinforced doors and the mount for the machine gun. Also note the original small driving mirrors, which would later be replaced by larger items.

An M1043 US Marine Corps armaments carrier. Note the flat surface of the doors, indicating that they carry supplemental armour. The armament in this variant is an M2 .50in machine gun. The hatch is open for loading ammunition and supplies, rather than hinged at the rear for access to ammunition when in action.

The M1037/M1042: S250 Shelter Carrier

Again the variants are numbered according to whether the vehicle carries a winch: M1037 without, M1042 with. The Standardized Integrated Command Post System Shelter (SICPS) is the basic structure for the Army's Advanced Tactical Command and Control System (ATCCS) which provides C4IEW and logistics support integration. The basic shelter is a six-sided box, made of aluminium facing panels bonded to a paper honeycomb core. There is space inside for two operators to use a variety of electronic equipment. As well as being mounted on a Humvee, the shelter may be ground-deployed. Additional tent-type extensions may be added to increase the capability of the shelter. To adapt an M998 into an S250 shelter carrier a shelter support, a shelter tailgate and a 200A umbilical power cable are required.

Four shelter reinforcement brackets secure the shelter to the vehicle. For transportation, a rear suspension tie-down kit is used to compress the rear suspension to maintain an overall height of 102in (259cm). The M1037 and M1042 shelter carriers are specifically designed to be operated with the S250 shelter installed and should not be driven for other than short distances without it fitted or the equivalent payload of 1,500lb (681kg). Long-distance driving without the payload will cause damage to the suspension.

The shelter originally fitted to the M1037/M1042 is an advanced version of the Lightweight Multi-Purpose Shelter (LMS) made by Marion Composites, a company involved in the military and aerospace business since the 1950s. For the required combination of lightness and strength, the Marion shelter is constructed of aluminium sheeting, joined by the patented folded and welded 'U-panel' construction on a WRII kraft paper honeycomb core. This material is strong enough to be drilled for shelving. The shelter provides protection against chemical and biological agents, employing a gas-particulate filtration and overpressure system. An advanced version offers on-board HVAC (heat, ventilation and air conditioning) and a power generator, providing a safe and secure shirt-sleeve environment for the occupants.

Shelter Dimensions

Exterior	84.0in (213cm) wide × 67.0in (170cm) high × 102.0in (259cm) long
Interior	81.5in (207cm) wide × 64.5in (164cm) high × 99.5in (253cm) long
Overall height on Prime Mover	102in (259cm)

Weight

Bare shelter	608lb (276kg)
Vehicle mounting kit	90lb (41kg)
Shelter payload	3,300lb (1,498kg)
Volume	285cu ft (8.07cu m)
Floor area (including wheel wells)	56sq ft (5.2sq m)
EMI-shielding	minimum of 60dB attenuation for electrical, magnetic and plane waves in frequency range 150kHz to 10GHz

Transportability

Air transport helicopter lift	conforms to MIL-M-8090, Type V
Drive-on/back-off cargo aircraft	up to 8mph (13km/h) rail impact
Floor loading	65lb/sq ft (317kg/sq m) overall, 500lb/sq ft (2,440kg/sq m), conforms to local MIL-STD-209H

Environmental

Rain	protection offered
Temperature, storage	−70° to +160°F (−57° to 71°C)
Temperature, operating	−65° to +125°F (−54° to 52°C)
Humidity	up to 100 per cent
Snow and ice	up to 5in/h (12.7cm/h), 40lb/sq ft (195kg/sq m)
Wind	up to 100mph (160km/h) steady (120mph [193km/h] gusts)

Two M1097 shelter carriers at Ram Jolly Firing Range, Camp Bondsteel, Kosovo.

Motors Powertrain Division developed a cleaner, more powerful 6.5ltr version to replace the 6.2. This produced 170bhp and 290lbft of torque. Additionally a new 4L80E electronically-controlled, four-speed automatic transmission would replace the old three-speed. Because the new engine and transmission would replace rather than supplement the old, AM General would have no choice but to fit the new powertrain, even though the delivery of the A1 variants had yet to be completed. As good as the 6.5ltr and four-speed was, it would mean that as any new Humvee was delivered two different engines would be found in service Humvees, a development which moved away from the ideal of complete standardization.

With new suspension components being fitted to the A1 variant, AM General, in co-operation with the military, took the positive step to incorporate the new powertrain into a second upgraded version. Further chassis improvements included larger 12in (30.5cm) brake discs all round, larger half-shafts, an improve steering wheel and column, a strengthened front cross-member, a new Warn military pattern 9,000lb (4,100kg) winch, improved vehicle tie-downs, a redesigned exhaust system with a catalytic converter and improved upper control arms and ball joints. Changes made to the interior included improved rear seats on the four-passenger version, sun visors and an improved heater. The engine had a new dual-voltage regulator/alternator system, a new air-cleaner element and an improved starter bracket. On the bodywork the capacity of the cargo mounts was increased to 2,500lb (1,135kg), the troop seats were made of a composite material, the windscreen retention fitting was improved, self-cancelling turn indicators were fitted, the driver's side mirror was relocated and new LED sidemarkers were fitted. Extra weather protection was built into the vehicle, including stainless steel brake and fuel lines, galvanized chassis rail and zinc-rich primer applied to the suspension components and chassis cross-members. The factory also fitted a kit to enable the installation of the Central Tire Inflation System (CTIS). Besides the original non-electronic system, an electronic system which automatically set the pressures of all four tyres to any one of four desired terrain conditions was available. Built into the electronic system was flat-tyre emergency mode. An LCD control panel, mounted on the engine tunnel, displayed tyre pressures and the operational selection.

The new model was numbered A2, according to established US military practice, and ten examples were delivered to the Army in April 1994. Delivery began in 1995, and the original and A1 variants would be phased out from then.

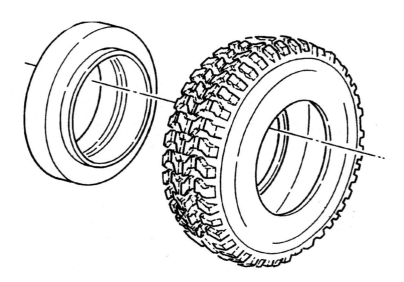

A2 variants were fitted with this simplified type of run-flat tyre, which has a solid rubber core.

M1097A2

Engine

Type	V8 diesel, liquid–cooled, naturally aspirated, EPA compliant
Capacity	6.5ltr (400cu in)
Bore and stroke	103 × 97mm (4.06 × 3.82in)
Compression ratio	21.3:1
Horsepower	160bhp (119kW) @ 3,400rpm
Torque	290lbft (393Nm) @ 1,700rpm
Electrical system	12/24V waterproof; 100 and 200A alternators available, 200A alternator standard on M997A2 and M1097A2

Transmission

Type	General Motors GM 4L80–E 4-speed Turbo-Hydramatic
Ratios	1st: 2.48:1, 2nd: 1.48:1, 3rd: 1.00:1, 4th 0.75:1, reverse 2.08:1
Transfer case	New Process NP242, 2-speed, full-time 4-wheel drive, ratios: high 1.01:1, low 2.72:1

Running Gear

Axles	suspended carrier, torque biasing hypoid differential, ratio 2.73:1 front and rear
Geared hubs	ratio 1.92:1
Brakes	hydraulically-actuated, 4-wheel inboard mounted power disc brakes with dual-reservoir master cylinder, 12.0in (30cm) rotors, mechanical parking brake operation on rear discs
Suspension	independent double A-frame with open-end coil springs, hydraulic shock absorbers
Steering	power-assisted with variable ratio of 13/16:1
Tyres	37 × 12.5 R16.5 LT load range 'D' radial with low-profile run-flat device
Wheels	16.5 × 8.25, 2-piece take-apart

Construction

Chassis	galvanized and E-coated steel box section with 5 cross-members
Bodywork	aluminium frame with aluminium panels

Dimensions (Basic M1097A2)

Length	4,840mm (190.4in)
Height	1,830mm (72in) to top of windscreen
Width	2,180mm (86in)
Wheelbase	3,302mm (130in)
Track, front and rear	1,819mm (71.6in)
Ground clearance	390mm (15.3in)
Fuel tank capacity	94.6ltr (25 US gals)

Performance

Maximum speed	113km/h (70mph)
Cruising range	520km (325 miles)
Acceleration	0–30mph (0–48km/h) 9.4sec (M1097A2, 6.5ltr turbo)
Maximum grade	60 per cent
Side slope operation	40 per cent (M1097A2 with shelter 30 per cent)
Approach angle	without winch: 63 degrees; with winch: 46 degrees
Departure angle	33 degrees
Maximum fording depth	normal: 760mm (30in); after preparation: 1,524mm (60in)
Turning circle	15.3m (50ft)

Air Transportability
Transportable in C-130 (3 HMMWVs); C-141E (6); C-5A (15); slung under CH-47 (2); CH-53 (2); UH-60 (1) (except M997A2 ambulance and armoured HMMWVs); all models except M997A2 ambulance may be deployed by conventional airdrop or Low Altitude Parachute Extraction System (LAPES); shelters must be removed from M1097A2 variants before airdrop or LAPES

Armament Provision
Mk19 40mm grenade machine gun, .50 cal M2HB or M2HB-QCB machine gun, Giat 20mm M621 cannon, M106 recoilless rifle, Giat 30mm M781 cannon, GAU-19 .50 cal 3-barrel Gatling gun, 7.62mm general purpose machine gun, 5.56mm general purpose machine gun, 30mm ASP-30 cannon, TOW and TOW II anti-tank missile systems, Mistral and Starburst anti-aircraft missile systems, Milan anti-armour missile system; M1113 variants are also designated as prime movers for M101, M102 and M119 howitzers

With its introduction, the Army took the opportunity to prune the number of variants and to renumber them with a simpler system. From the original seventeen numbers in service with both the Army and the Marines, there would be just six. The complexity created by giving different numbers to otherwise identical models because they were or were not fitted with a winch would cease. Now the winch was regarded as something that could be installed on, or removed from, any variant that required or was authorized to have one. All models that were originally designated as having a winch lost their number. For example, the M1025 weapons carrier without winch and the M1026 weapons carrier with winch which had been numbered as M1025A1 and M1026A1, respectively, were incorporated under the single number M1025A2. The original M998/M1038 and the M998A1/M1038A1 would be phased out and replaced by the M1097A2 variants. The M996 and M996A1 TOW missile carrier with basic Kevlar armour would not remain in service, nor would it be replaced by an A2 variant. Also dropped would be the M966 mini ambulance.

The A2 variants would be:

M1097A2 Cargo/Troop/Shelter Carrier
M1045A2 TOW Missile Carrier with Supplemental Armour
M1025A2 Armament Carrier Armoured
M1043A2 Armament Carrier Armoured (US Marines)

M997A2 Maxi Ambulance
M1035A2 Soft Top Ambulance

The M1043A2 would also be used by the Military Police. Weapons carrier variants could be fitted with the standard M2 .50 calibre machine gun, a 30mm ASP-30 auto cannon, or a .50- calibre GAU-19/A 3-barrel Gatling gun. The A2's new bumpers made the vehicles slightly longer and other modifications altered the overall vehicle dimensions. These affected its approach angle, shipping dimensions and special winch-assisted operations. The mandatory radial-ply tyres extended the cruising range of all variants by approximately 30 miles (48km).

A2 models can be fitted with arctic heaters for use in temperatures from 0°F (-18°C) to -50°F (-46°C). M997A2 ambulance interior lighting systems were designed so that all white-light illumination in the patient compartment would be extinguished when the bulkhead doors, rear doors or rear steps were opened, unless the vehicle main light switch was in 'SERVICE DRIVE' position. In 2000 the M1097A2 was given fifteen-year corrosion protection.

Special Versions

AM General produced a number of special versions of the M1097A2, some of which were for sale beyond the USA. These included a right-hand-drive version, a wrecker, a field maintenance vehicle, a Mistral missile carrier, a firefighting model and a Starburst missile carrier. The up-armoured M1097A1 was carried over as an A2 variant.

The M1113 Expanded Capacity Humvee

The M1109's extra load limited its payload to 1,300lb (590kg), which was well below the 2,200lb (999kg) specified in the original HMMWV programme. In 1994 AM General developed a cab-over Humvee (COHHV, *see* Chapter 9) which had a much higher payload and uprated suspension. Power was from a tur-

bocharged version of the 6.5ltr diesel, producing 190bhp, some 30bhp more than the naturally aspirated 6.5ltr, and an impressive 380lbft of torque, an almost 25 per cent improvement.

A further development was the Expanded Capability Vehicle (ECV). This had a conventional layout with the strengthened chassis, modified steering system, new rear exhaust, 3.08:1 ratio differentials, half-shafts and larger 12in (30.5cm) brake discs, improved cooling system and the one-piece wheels with run-flat tyres of the cab-over variant. These modifications raised the payload from 4,400 to 5,300lb (2,000 to

An M1045A2 belonging to the Danish armed forces. The A2 differs visually from the A1 in two ways; the driver's side mirror is placed lower and the tie-down brackets, oval in shape, are placed further out than on previous models. The original fixings for the old tie-down brackets are still fitted.

BELOW: An up-armoured M1025A1 of the United Arab Emirates Army serving with KFOR in Kosovo in 2000. This armoured variant may be identified by the shield over the air intake on the bonnet, the protruding windows and the horizontal, slatted grill. The armour plate is noticeable on the body just behind the front wheel. (CTIS is fitted to this vehicle).

2,400kg), with an increased kerb weight of 6,200lb (2,815kg) and GVW of 11,500lb (5,220kg). The higher payload demanded the use of new wheel rims, which would become standardized on all Humvees. Power came from the COHHV's 6.5ltr V8 turbo diesel. Even then the engine would have to do some hard work, and, to help it, the differential ratio was dropped to 3.08:1, bringing the armoured vehicle's official acceleration figures in line with that of the unarmoured variants. Air conditioning was factory installed. CTIS was also factory-fitted, the ECV being the first Humvee variant so supplied. The ECV was given the generic number M1113 and was available as a basic, stripped-out variant suitable for mounting several equipment and body variants.

Fully Armoured Variants

The higher potential payload of the M1113 enabled O'Gara Hess and Eisenhardt in 1993 to mount the body of the up-armoured XM1109 on to the new chassis. The body could be supplied in square or slant-back form, according to the needs of the user. The body armour offered full 360-degree occupant protection from 7.62mm AP rounds. Armouring for the bonnet was available, and additional underbody panels provided protection for the crew against landmines.

M1114 and M1115

O'Gara Hess and Eisenhardt were chosen to develop further armoured versions on the ECV chassis. Two variants were envisaged: the M1114 armament carrier and the M1115 TOW carrier. Naturally the weight of armour increased the M1113's GVW of 11,500lb (5,220kg) by 600lb (272kg) to 12,100lb (5,493kg). Thus, while the total laden weight of both the M1113 and M1114 remained the same, the armour would reduce the payload of the M1114 by 600lb to 2,300lb (1,044kg). O'Gara Hess and Eisenhardt sent the XM1114 prototype to the US Army in September 1995. The chassis components being of an existing approved type, the focus of attention was on the armour. By December ballistic blast testing was carried out on the XM1114 at the US Army Proving Grounds in Aberdeen, Maryland. It passed and the M1114 was ready to

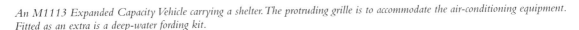

An M1113 Expanded Capacity Vehicle carrying a shelter. The protruding grille is to accommodate the air-conditioning equipment. Fitted as an extra is a deep-water fording kit.

The M1114. The protruding grille is to accommodate the turbocharger. Note also the louvres on the slant-back.

go into service. There was no requirement for a fully armoured TOW missile carrier, and so M1115 remained just a number. It would not be long before the M1114 saw action, for in March 1996 the first examples were shipped to Bosnia for peacekeeping duties in the civil war.

The M1114 offered greater protection than the up-armoured M1109, especially in the close-quarter work undertaken in peacekeeping missions in an urban environment, where rules of engagement might limit the opportunity to begin or even retaliate in a firefight. The armour minimizes the possible casualties from 12lb-contact-detonated anti-tank mines in the front of the vehicle and 4lb-contact-detonated land mines at the rear, 7.62mm armour-piercing rounds and artillery fire that could be encoun-

tered in high-risk operations such as these. The doors can resist 7.62mm AP rounds from 100m (109yd) and have 'white glass' transparent armour windows that can be lowered to act as an arms port. The windscreen, which is also of 'white glass', contains an electric de-icing system. The roof overlaps the top of the body sides and is mounted on shock-absorbing bushes. It provides protection from a 155mm overhead burst from 100m. The turret can mount either M2 or M60 machine guns or a Mk19 grenade launcher. Production of the M1114 continued from 1994; the 500th example was delivered in November 1996, the 1,000th following in May 1998. In April 2000 the US Army awarded O'Gara Hess and Eisenhardt a further five-year contract for M1114s.

An M1114 belonging to the US Military Police, serving with KFOR in Kosovo in 2000. The weapon carried is a Mk19 40mm grenade launcher.

M1113/M1114

Engine: All Variants

Type	V8 diesel, liquid-cooled, turbocharged, EPA-compliant
Capacity	6.5ltr (400cu in)
Bore and stroke	103 × 97mm (4.06 × 3.82in)
Compression ratio	21.3:1
Horsepower	190bhp (142kW) @ 3,400rpm
Torque	380lbft (515Nm) @1,700rpm
Electrical system	12/24V waterproof, 100 and 200A alternators available; 200A alternator standard on M997A2 and M1097A2

Transmission: All Variants

Type	4-speed automatic
Ratios	1st: 2.48:1, 2nd: 1.48:1, 3rd: 1.00:1, 4th: 0.75:1, reverse 2.08:1
Transfer case	New Process NP242, 2-speed, full-time 4-wheel drive, ratios: high 1.01:1, low 2.72:1

Running Gear: All Variants

Axles	suspended carrier, torque biasing hypoid differential, ratio 3.08:1 front and rear
Geared hubs	ratio 1.92:1

Weights, Dimensions and Performance: M1113

Dimensions

Length	5m (196.5in)
Height (without weapons)	1.88m (74in)
Minimum reducible height	1.42m (56in)

Weights

Kerb weight	2,858kg (6,302lb)
Payload	2,317kg (5,109lb)
GVW	5,216kg (11,500lb)

Performance

0–30mph (0–48km/h)	9.4sec
0–50mph (0–80km/h)	26.1sec
Maximum towed load	1,890kg (4,167lb)
Cruising range, minimum	443km (275 miles)
Seating capacity	driver + 1

Weights, Dimensions and Performance: M1114

Dimensions

Length	5m (196.5in)
Height (without weapons)	1.88m (74in)
Minimum reducible height	1.83m (72in)
Ground clearance	0.38m (15in)

Weights

Kerb weight	4,445kg (9,800lb)
Payload	1,043kg (2,300lb)
GVW	5,489kg (12,100lb)

Performance

0–30mph (0–48km/h)	6.96sec
Maximum towed load	2,041kg (4,500lb)
Cruising range, minimum	443km (275 miles)
Seating capacity	driver + 3

Armour Protection
7.62mm armour-piercing rounds, 155mm overhead airburst, 12lb anti-tank mines, 4lb front and rear underbody blast

The nature of the vehicle, based on a platform shared with soft-skinned variants, enabled forces equipped with them to respond efficiently. In emergencies the response needs be to quick and the nature of them often means that only a limited amount of equipment can be shipped. The conditions encountered in such situations confirm the wisdom of standardization of the degree attained in the Humvee. When some of your most useful fighting vehicles use the same spare parts as your battlefield support and general service utility vehicles, the amount of *matériel* you need to move by air is considerably reduced. You can spare more space for troops or get the same force there with fewer aircraft, reducing both the cost and the time taken in shipping.

M1116

The Security Forces Squadrons of the US Air force, charged with the defence of air bases, had a need for a highly mobile, armoured, rapid response vehicle to guard against intruders and to protect the base resources. In May 1998 they took delivery of their own version of the up-armoured Humvee, the M1116. It has an expanded cargo area in a square-back form, an armoured housing for the turret-gun operator and an enhanced interior heat and air circulation system. The M1116 provides ballistic protection against 7.62mm AP ammunition and against overhead projectiles and protection against underbelly grenade and mine fragmentation attack and blast.

The inside of the M1116's armoured doors.

The 6.5ltr turbocharged engine in the M1116 is hidden below the pipework for the turbocharger and the air-conditioning equipment.

A four-man crew is carried in the M1116 along with their personal equipment and their weapons, ammunition, chemical-protection gear, bomb-disposal clothing and up to 1,200lb (545kg) of cargo. The gun platform in the 360 degree, manual-drive, armour-protected turret can accommodate a Mk19 grenade launcher, M2 and M60 machine guns or an M-82A1 Barret .50-calibre rifle. Unexploded 'smart' cluster bombs that can detect the presence of a vehicle or personnel can be deployed to render an airfield runway unserviceable; the Barret rifle is used to explode such bombs from a safe distance.

Despite having smaller windows and windscreen, the visibility from inside the M1116 is at an acceptable level. Far from being an encumbrance, the cover over the drivetrain makes a suitable elevated platform for the gunner.

BELOW: *The M1116 is exclusive to the USAF. This example is based at RAF Lakenheath.*

7 Further Developments – Up-Armour and Other Variants

Now entering its third decade of existence, the Humvee has established itself as a truly versatile vehicle for the US Armed forces. Its original form has found applications in overseas markets including Abu Dhabi, Algeria, Bahrain, Bolivia, Chad, China, Colombia, Denmark, Djibouti, Ecuador, Egypt, Greece, Honduras, Israel, Japan, Jordan, Kuwait, Luxembourg, Mexico, Morocco, the Philippines, Qatar, Saudi Arabia, Switzerland, Taiwan, Thailand, Tunisia, Turkey and Venezuela. Foreign manufacturers have also developed variants for their own countries' use and for further markets.

Up-Armoured Variants

We have seen that, at its inception, the Humvee was developed to fulfil four roles: as a light truck, a light armaments carrier, a shelter carrier and an ambulance. In addition, variants have been developed that both take the concept of the armoured car almost back to its roots and bring it fully up to date. During the Great War the Royal Naval Air Service used armour-clad Rolls-Royce and Napier cars as fast reconnaissance vehicles on the Western Front, and later the Royal Air Force used similar vehicles to counter rebel activities in the Middle East. The armoured car has been a favoured tool of authorities world-wide to control civil disturbances. The concept was developed further by the Hungarian engineer Nicholas Straussler, whose vehicle, with a separate chassis, was produced by the British fighting vehicle manufacturer Alvis. During World War II the M8 Staghound armoured car was built by Ford on a separate chassis, and unit construction armoured cars, or armoured reconnaissance vehicles, as they became known, were produced in Britain, by Daimler.

MOWAG Eagle

The MOWAG Eagle takes the principle of the armoured car some way back to its origins by building an up-armoured body on a Heavy Hummer chassis. The Swiss engineer Walter Ruf founded the MOWAG (Motorwagenfabrik AG) company in Kreuzlingen in Switzerland in 1950 as a private venture to produce high-tech, specialized, military vehicles. These include: the Piranha series of four-, six- and eight-wheeled armoured personnel carriers (APCs); the Tornado tracked APC and the Grenadier and the Roland series of wheeled APCs. The entire range has been available for export, and a number of countries, including Germany, manufactured particular models under licence. MOWAG remained in Ruf's sole ownership until 1999, when he sold out to General Motors of Canada. GM subsequently incorporated MOWAG into their Defence Operations Division.

The development of MOWAG's Eagle 4×4 began in 1993, with the delivery of 156 examples to the Swiss armed forces in 1995. The Eagle carries an armoured superstructure of MOWAG's own making on the M1097A2 Heavy Hummer chassis and uses its 6.5ltr, naturally-aspirated V8 diesel engine and four-speed automatic transmission. It is of a similar configuration to AM General's original weapons carrier variants, having four doors and a rear cargo

Despite having a totally different body from that built by O'Gara, Hess and Eisenhardt for the M1114/5/6 series, MOWAG's Eagle clearly shows that it is a Humvee variant. This version is ready for dispatch to the Danish Military Police and mounts a turret on the roof for a machine gun and smoke-canister launchers. Note the profile of the body sides, which account for its extra width.

hatch. In addition, a circular roof hatch is provided over the commander's seat. Described as being 'ideally suited for reconnaissance, surveillance, liaison, escort, border patrol and police missions', it features an armoured superstructure with armoured glass windows and windscreen. Located in the centre of the roof, a MOWAG MBK2 armoured observation cupola can rotate through 360 degrees and has a thermal-imaging unit to allow all-round operation, by day or night and in all weather conditions. Armament is a 7.62mm machine gun, which is mounted on the cupola and may be elevated to 20 degrees and depressed by 12 degrees. Banks of six smoke grenade dischargers are mounted at the front and the rear of the turret.

MOWAG maintain that the armour and the cupola, which add about a metric tonne (0.98 ton) to that of the basic M1097A2, do not compromise its performance. The Eagle 4×4 is NBC-tight and provides individual, comfortably upholstered seats for four. Although the composite armour-plate body makes the Eagle heavier and 100mm (3.9in) wider than the original Hummer, the vehicle is still air-transportable by C–130 aircraft or helicopter.

The MOWAG Eagle II on test. Note the larger glass in comparison with the MkI.

MOWAG Eagle 4×4 MRI

Engine
Type   General Motors normally-aspirated V8 Diesel
Capacity   6.5ltr (399.75cu in)
Power   160bhp (117kW) @ 3,400rpm
Torque   393Nm @ 1,700rpm

Gearbox
Type   4 L 80 E Hydra-Matic
Gear ratios   1st: 2.48:1, 2nd: 1.48:1, 3rd: 1.00:1, 4th: 0.75:1, reverse: 2.08:1
Transfer case   New Venture NP218 dual-range with permanent four-wheel drive
Ratios   high: 1:1, low: 2.72:1

Running Gear
Suspension   independent wheel suspension with double control arms
Axles   with torsion differential
Brakes   inboard disc brakes for all four wheels
Tyres   37 × 12.50 R 16.5 LT run-flat

Electrical System
Voltage   24V
Alternator   24V, 100A
Battery   24V, 125Ah

Weights
Weight unladen   3,800kg (8,380lb)
Payload   1,000kg (2,200lb)
Total combat weight   4,800kg (10,580lb)

Dimensions
Overall length   490cm (193in)
Height over hull   175cm (69in)
Overall width   228cm (90in)
Wheelbase   330cm (130in)
Wheel track (front, rear) 181cm (71in)
Ground clearance   40cm (16in)
Angle of approach   60 degrees
Angle of departure   50 degrees
Number of seats   4/5

Performance
Maximum speed   125km/h (78mph)
Maximum speed, reverse 35km/h (22mph)
Gradient   60 per cent
Side slope   40 per cent
Turning circle diameter 14.6m (48ft)
Fuel tank capacity   95ltr (25 US gal)
Range on hard level surface 450km (280 miles)
Fording depth   0.76m (2.5ft)

Alamein in 1942. Working in small units, they used specially adapted jeeps, heavily armed and with an engine cooling system of increased capacity to cope with the desert, one of the hottest places on earth.

Whatever the nature of the job, sabotage or reconnaissance, the troops engaged on it need to get to the target and out again quickly. There is a need for light machine weapons, and a Special Operations vehicle can provide the platform for

these. Because of the Humvee's high payload and superb off-road ability, it is seen as an ideal vehicle for such operations and AM General produce such a variant. Mounted on Humvees, the US Special Forces played a crucial role in destroying Iraqi air-defence systems in the Gulf War. Other nations looked at the Humvee for the role of fast surveillance vehicle, either modified or as the base for a new variant.

ABOVE: A special operations vehicle, stripped of all superstructure except half-height doors. The M1 .50-calibre machine gun is carried on a lightweight weapons station kit.

The Trackvee. Bolt-on tracks fitted to this M1025A1 have been used in many occasions on the past on such vehicles as the Jeep, the MUTT and the M715. Note the snorkel for the deep-water fording kit, which is standard equipment on US Marine vehicles.

Project *Mulgara*

A tiny marsupial, the mulgara might be described as Australia's own 'desert rat', so that it was apt for the Australian Army to adopt the name in 1994 when it began looking for a light surveillance and reconnaissance vehicle (LSRV) for its needs in the twenty-first century. Project *Mulgara's* specifications demanded a light vehicle with an unladen weight of 1.5 tonnes (1.48 tons), a payload of 1.2 tonnes (1.18 tons) and a GVW of 2.7 tonnes (2.66 tons). The four-wheel-drive vehicle then in service, the Land Rover-derived Perentie, had a payload of 1.2 tonnes (1.18 tons) and an unladen weight of between 2.2 and 2.4 tonnes (2.17–2.36 tons). A comparison shows that this specification was much lighter than that of the Humvee, but none the less, GM Holden's Special Vehicle division was selected to prepare a number of Humvees for the tender at their Clayton, Victoria, plant.

In two regards the Humvee met the specification: those of ground clearance and climbing ability. *Mulgara* demanded 350mm (13.8in); the Humvee 406mm (16.0in). Although its departure angle of 37.5 degrees was a little shy of the specification figure of 50, its approach of angle of 72 degrees was quite close to the 75 demanded. So was its ability to handle a vertical obstacle of 450mm (17.7in).

The demand that the new vehicle should be able to accelerate from 0 to 100km/h (0 to 62mph) in less than 20sec could be met, as could a minimum cruising speed of 90km/h (56mph). Run-flat tyres and diesel engine, also demanded, were already in place. A maximum of 200kg (440lb) of armour for small-arms and anti-personnel mine protection was also listed, and such protection had at the time been fitted to the M1097.

The deadline for submissions was November 1995, and over a dozen from firms in Australia, New Zealand, South Africa, the United Kingdom, the USA and Japan were received. The tenders were finally in by the middle of 1996, ready for testing that would last until 1998. A small number of applicants were to be selected in 1997 and asked to submit trial vehicles for an exhaustive testing programme in 1998. However, politics forced a change following the 1996 federal elections, when the Australian defence forces came under a major review. Project *Mulgara* was cancelled in October 1997. The 500 vehicles that might have been ordered were no longer wanted.

Alvis Shadow

British Special Forces have used specially equipped 'Pink Panther' Land Rovers, but by the end of the 1990s these vehicles were due for

The Shadow, an ultra-lightweight special body of square-tube construction, literally bristles with armaments. Its square-tube superstructure is mounted on a Humvee chassis. In comparison with the special operations vehicle on page 95, it is narrower and the driving position is slightly further forward. Note also the rear-facing seat just behind the powertrain cover.

AM General also make a 1-ton trailer for use behind the Humvee.

BELOW: A right-hand-drive version of the M1097 is available to those countries that require it. This view shows the space available in the cargo bed and the newer type of seat.

ABOVE: *An M1025 in its element, off the beaten track. Terrain like this is easy for a Humvee.*

The geared reduction hub, fitted with CTIS. The hub is drilled through its centre and air is pumped or let out of the tyre through the black rubber pipe in the centre. The solid rubber run-flat insert can also be seen.

replacement. In 1994 the British Ministry of Defence sent out a specification for a new type of long-range deep-penetration vehicle. Alvis Vehicles Ltd of Coventry, long established in the field of fighting vehicles with the FV600 and CVR(T) series, won the contract to develop the vehicle, known as the Shadow. They entered into partnership with Reumech of South Africa and used that company's Cheko A-Wagen chassis and square-tube superstructure. It was powered by a GM petrol engine and four-speed Hydramatic gearbox. The engine was soon changed to a GM 6.5ltr turbo diesel, while retaining the GM gearbox. Brakes were outboard of the all-independent, coil-spring suspension. Some time after 1996, following trials, the project was scrapped.

A new version, the Shadow Offensive Action Vehicle, was unveiled at the annual AUSA (Association of the US Army) Show, held in Washington, DC, in October 2000. It was based on the M1113 Expanded Capacity Humvee chassis, but the vehicle was 6in (152mm) narrower and 9in (229mm) shorter. The superstructure was a new version of the original, modified to fit the Humvee chassis. This reduced the weight below that of the basic Humvee, allowing two Shadows to be carried in CH-47 and CH-53 helicopters. Its advantage over the Land Rover was said to be its extended range and larger payload capacity.

Thanks to its all-round independent suspension, as against the Land Rover's live axles, the Shadow was also claimed to have a greater off-road mobility and reliability. Further, the British Army was moving to one fuel, diesel. Rover at the time could offer only a petrol V8 with enough power to cope with the payload, whereas the Shadow had the Humvee's diesel V8. Unfortunately, this later version of the Shadow was also abandoned.

AM General Acquire General Motors' V8 Diesel Engine

AM General and its predecessors had been doing business with General Motors for a long time. Kaiser Industries, when it owned Jeep, bought Buick's old V6 for use in the CJ-5 and used Hydra-Matic transmissions and the new Buick cast-iron V8 in the Wagoneer and the Gladiator. The American Motors Corporation, AM General's then parent company, bought in Pontiac four-cylinder petrol engines for Jeeps and Concord passenger cars, and four-cylinder diesels from GM's Japanese Isuzu subsidiary in the 1980s for use in the Jeep CJ-7 and CJ-8. New Process Gear, which supplied transfer cases for Jeeps and the Hummer, was a jointly-owned subsidiary of General Motors and Chrysler, and GM's Power-

The AN-TSC 93B tactical satellite communication system mounted on an M1097A1. This vehicle is operated by the New York-based Marine Reserve, 6th Communications Battalion in direct support of the Baltic Challenge exercise in Paldiski, Estonia in 1997.

train Division's (formerly Detroit Diesel Allison's) V8 diesel was the heart of AM General's HMMWV. When the LTV Aerospace and Defense group acquired AM General, the relationship with GM continued.

Now GM planned the eventual closure of the Moraine, Ohio plant in 2000, where it built, among other engines, the V8 diesel. Although it would make sufficient numbers for its own needs until 2002, the logical step was for AM General

---

Amtech Hard Tops

The US manufacturer Amtech are specialists in glassfibre and other plastic mouldings for industrial and domestic use. They designed and produced this glassfibre hard top for the Humvee. It provides a weatherproof cover for sensitive electronic equipment and for tools that might otherwise be damaged by rain. It also has a low profile, which is an advantage over the conventional SICPS shelters when moving across country in a combat situation.

A 1987 ex-USAF M998 in private hands, fitted with a fibreglass hard top by the Amtech Corporation. These vehicles are used by tactical air control parties for calling in air strikes in support of ground troops. The top has hard points for mounting antennas, the roof is reinforced for a 500lb (227kg) load and the centre has a copper screen to work with the antennae. The toolboxes on each side hold cable reels, antennas and accessories.

This M1097A1 photographed at the Ram Jolly Firing Range in Kosovo also has an Amtech hard top. This particular vehicle, which was being used as a general utility vehicle, belongs to the 1st Infantry (Mechanized) Division, US Army, but was actually in the custody of the 1st Armored Division who were in the process of replacing 1st Infantry. Similar vehicles are used by commanding officers in the field. It is not known whether the Pepsi-Cola cans in the rear have any tactical significance.

received the order to begin the operation on the next day with a D-Day and H-hour of 20 December, 0100 local. The limited military objectives in Plan *90-2* were: to protect American lives, key sites and facilities; capture and deliver Noriega to a competent authority; neutralize the PDF's command and control and eventually to restructure the PDF; and support the establishment of a government in Panama that could be recognized by the USA.

On 20 December the paratroops designated for participation in what was now named Operation *Just Cause* were dispatched from Forts Bragg, Benning and Stewart in a fleet of 148 aircraft. The airports in Panama were the first targets, with units from the 75th Ranger Regiment and the 82nd Airborne Division conducting airborne assaults at Rio Hato and Torrijos/Tocumen airports, and the 82nd landing on to Torrijos International Airport.

LEFT: *The blackened building bears witness to the close-quarter fighting that took place in Panama City. Here, US troops patrol the city streets in an M1026.*

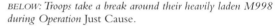

BELOW: *Troops take a break around their heavily laden M998 during Operation* Just Cause.

The 1st Brigade Task Force made up of the 1st and 2nd Battalion, 504th Parachute Infantry Regiment, parachuted into combat for the first time since World War II. In Panama the paratroopers were joined on the ground by the 3rd Battalion, which was already in Panama. After the night combat jump and seizure of the airport, the 82nd conducted follow-on combat air-assault missions in Panama City and the surrounding areas. They were followed later by the 2nd and 1st Brigade of the 7th Infantry Division. Already in Panama were the 3rd Brigade, the 7th Infantry Division, the 193rd Infantry Brigade and 4th/6th Infantry Division, the 5th Infantry Division and the 504th Parachute Infantry Regiment. These, with the exception of the 3rd Battalion of the 504th, who were with the troops involved in capturing the airports, moved on to objectives in Panama City and on the Atlantic side of the Canal. All D-Day objectives were secured by the first day. As units moved to their new objectives the 7th Infantry Division moved into the western areas of Panama and on to Panama City.

The fighting in Panama City was extremely difficult. In such close-quarter engagements it is hard for forces to recognize their own people and to identify the enemy, who may be holed up in tall buildings. The troops in Operation *Just Cause* learned some hard lessons about the secondary effects of weapons in close-quarter fighting in an urban battleground. To the regret of the US military and the government, hundreds of Panamanian lives were lost and there was subsequent damage to Panama City and El Chorillo. Nevertheless, the American troops involved achieved their primary objectives quickly, and troop withdrawal began on 27 December. Noriega eventually surrendered to the US authorities voluntarily. He is now serving a forty-year sentence in Florida for drug trafficking.

Operations *Desert Shield* and *Desert Storm*

It would be more than seven years after AM General received the initial contract for the Humvee that the vehicle would gain its first large-scale combat experience. It would be in a desert environment, as part of the Gulf War.

Iraq and Iran had been at war for seven years, engaged in a bloody and hateful campaign but which showed no signs of victory for either side. Iran, under the Muslim fundamentalist government of Ayatollah Khomeni, faced the no less despotic Iraqi regime of Saddam Hussein. The war was crippling Iraq financially. By 1990 the national debt was rapidly outstripping oil revenues. Saddam could not keep this up and hope to stay in power, although he had enough force at his disposal to quash any and all internal dissent. From Iraq's point of view, a much quicker means to secure victory, or, at the very least, peace with honour, was essential.

Iraqi opposition parties in exile combined to condemn Saddam, and the arrest, torture and subsequent execution of the British reporter Fazad Bazoft on a spying charge began to focus worldwide attention on the country. The involvement of the British firm of Matrix-Churchill in the 'Supergun' affair, when major components for the weapon were seized before they reached Iraq, drew attention to Saddam's intention to use his considerable chemical and biological weaponry on neighbouring states, possibly Israel.

Saddam considered himself to be the champion of the Arab world, a latter-day Saladin. He cited Israel as a potential invader and a tool through which the USA would undermine the Arab cause. Saddam believed that, in opposing this perceived threat from Israel, he would unite the Arab world and get them to help him out of his financial crisis.

In an Arab summit in May 1990 Saddam tried to bring his aspirations to fulfilment. Instead, a boycott of the summit by Syria caused great anxiety, not only to Egypt but also to Iraq's close neighbours, Saudi Arabia and the small Gulf states to the south. But not only did the rest of the Arab world refuse to offer Saddam aid, but a decline in the price of crude oil made matters much worse. The price drop was attributed to high production, and Saddam decided that two countries in particular were to blame: the United Arab Emirates and Kuwait. After failing to persuade either to reduce their output, Saddam condemned them for their so-called treachery and implied that he would take some kind of military action.

Neither Kuwait, the UAE nor indeed the USA believed that he would resort to military action. Through his Secretary of State James Baker, President Bush pursued a programme of 'shuttle diplomacy' to try to resolve the situation. Saddam would not budge. He accused Kuwait of 'stealing' oil to the value of $2.4 million from the Rumailah oilfield that lay under the land on either side of the border between the two countries; and when Kuwait had the temerity to remind Iraq that the interest on the loans it had made was due, Saddam moved. On 2 August 1990 he invaded Kuwait.

The Arab League condemned the invasion, and the UN Security Council adopted Resolution 660, sending the same message of condemnation to Saddam. The USA urged the introduction of economic sanctions against Iraq, which resulted in the backing of such a move by Resolution 661; but it soon became clear that only force would free Kuwait. Six days after the Iraqi Army first moved on Kuwait, Bush announced that American ground troops would be sent to Saudi Arabia to defend against a possible invasion by Iraq. The carrier USS *Independence* had already been dispatched

on 30 July to the Gulf, and two squadrons of F-15 fighters were put on standby for deployment in the area. Operation *Desert Shield* had begun.

The build-up of ground forces began on 7 August, with the deployment of the 82nd Airborne Division and the 101st Air Assault Division. Special forces and an armoured division arrived from Syria, as well as Special Forces from Morocco. Under the command of Headquarters, XVIII Corps 2 Brigades of the 1st Cavalry Division, the 24th Mechanized Infantry Division, the 3rd Armored Cavalry Regiment and the XVIII Corps Artillery, joined them in September and October, swelling the number of American troops to 25,000.

In November, under Headquarters, VII Corps, the existing US forces were bolstered by the 1st and 3rd Armored Division, the 1st Infantry division, the 2nd Armored Cavalry Regiment, three brigades of the VII Corps Artillery, the 11th Combat Aviation Brigade, two brigades of the III Corps Artillery, the 7th Air Defense Artillery Brigade, the 11th Air Defense Artillery Brigade, the 12th Combat Aviation Brigade, the 5th Special Forces Group and the 227th Aviation Regiment. In addition to the Army personnel, there were also the 1st Marine Expeditionary Force and the 13th Marine Expeditionary Unit ashore,

An M1026 armaments carrier. The US Special Forces who used this particular vehicle refer to it as a desert mobility vehicle (DMV). Although this particular picture was taken after Operation Desert Storm during an exercise at the National Training Center, the vehicle is still in desert colours and all the camouflage netting is carried.

as well as the 2nd Marine Division, including the 4th and 5th Marine Expeditionary Brigade's Divisional Artillery and Divisional Aviation afloat in the Mediterranean.

In Washington, DC, overall military control of the rapidly forming International Coalition was under Gen Colin Powell, chairman of the Joint Chiefs of Staff, but on the ground, CENTCOM, the US Central Command, was under Gen Norman Schwarzkopf. A big man in every sense, Schwarzkopf is known to his colleagues as 'the Bear', a nickname he much prefers to that given to him by the media, 'Stormin' Norman'. Clearly the bulk of the fighting force was American, but in close support, and creating the second largest partner in the Coalition, was the British Army. There was the 1st Armoured Division, including the 7th Armoured Brigade, the successor to the famous Desert Rats of the North African campaign of World War II, the Armoured Reconnaissance Regiment, the Royal Marines and elements of the Special Air Service Regiment and the Special Boat Squadron. The RAF provided Tornado low-level attack and Jaguar strike aircraft. All British forces were under the command of Lt Gen Sir Peter de la Billière, who himself was second to Gen Schwarzkopf.

Of notable political significance were a chemical defence unit from the former Warsaw Pact country, Czechoslovakia and two army divisions from Egypt. Other nations supplying a total of 18,000 troops for *Desert Shield* were Bangladesh, Senegal, Nigeria and Pakistan. In addition, France, Italy and Canada supplied attack, reconnaissance and support aircraft.

When the build-up was complete, the coalition troops totalled 200,000, with 1,900 tanks, 930 artillery pieces and 456 attack helicopters. They faced an estimated Iraqi force of close on half a million men. Although the Coalition was heavily outnumbered, most of the equipment it possessed was up-to-date, whereas the Iraqi Army's hardware was ageing badly, and poorly maintained at that. All of the Coalition troops were regular servicemen and women, while a high percentage of the Iraqi Army was made up of conscripts and veteran reservists.

Those troops were not in place simply to defend Saudi Arabia. They were there to drive Saddam's forces out of Kuwait if he would not pull them out under diplomatic pressure. But to attack, to send American troops into battle, Bush needed the authority of Congress. It was not long in coming, thanks to Saddam's own twisted logic. He captured

Operation Desert Storm. *This is a typical arrangement of a communications station, set between the driver and the vehicle commander positions in an M1026 DMV (desert mobility vehicle). On the top of the stack is an encryption device, connected to an encrypted VHF radio. Below the VHF radio is an HF radio for long-distance communication. Hanging from the roof is the GPS. The square padded container to the right holds the commander's PVS-7 night-vision goggles. In front of the goggles is the commander's Walkman – no personal radios or CD players are installed. One of the trucks in the detachment would carry a satellite radio. This is more reliable than HF, which is relegated to back-up status. If expected to work with fixed-wing air support, the vehicles would carry a UHF radio.*

many foreign nationals, including women, children and old people, whom he placed at strategic sites as 'human shields'. What reluctance there was among the American people to see outright war largely evaporated at the sight of these hostages shown on Iraqi television. Bush got, by a narrow margin, Congressional authority to launch the relief of Kuwait – Operation *Desert Storm*.

Desert Storm would be in two parts. The first would be to gain as complete a control of the air and of the airwaves as possible by wiping out as much of the Iraqi air-defence and command systems. This would principally be by air attack, through strike aircraft and cruise missiles launched from both Saudi Arabian territory and from American ships. In addition, the Iraqis' ability to repair the damage and resupply their troops had to be crushed.

Air attacks started on 17 January 1991. CNN journalists in the Al-Rashid Hotel in Baghdad were astonished to see cruise missiles flying at street level and actually turning corners to reach their targets. Within hours many of Iraq's radar systems had been wiped out. Without them, the Iraqi SAM (surface to air missile) system was effectively shooting blind, even when the operators had any warning of Coalition aircraft. Only

simple anti-aircraft gunnery had any chance of shooting down Coalition planes. B-52 bombers dropped hundreds of tons of explosives on Iraqi troops, sheltering, if they were lucky, in bunkers in the Kuwaiti desert.

Iraq had one weapon that caused concern not only in the Coalition, but also in Israel – the Scud missile. The main danger of this Soviet-made, medium-range weapon was that it could carry, if Iraq had developed the technology far enough, either chemical or biological weapons. Its range of between 100 and 170 miles (160 and 274km) put Israel's major cities of Tel Aviv and Haifa, and the Saudi capital Riyadh, in Saddam's sights. Launched from either a permanent site or from the back of a heavy truck, the Scud was not only dangerous but in its mobile form difficult to trace. The first Scud was launched on Israel on the morning of the first Coalition attack, 18 January, and many others followed, fired at both Israel and Saudi Arabia. Retaliation by Israel would surely escalate the war by bringing in Syria and Jordan on Iraq's side, and the Israelis' were only dissuaded from direct involvement by Bush's fulfilled promise of the deployment of American Patriot missiles in Israel. It was indeed fortunate that the attacks resulted in only a small number of civilian deaths and injuries.

A US Marine Corps M1044 armed with an Mk19 automatic grenade launcher sits beside a motorcycle beneath a camouflage net at the 1st Battalion, 5th Marines Combat Operations Center (COC) during Operation Desert Shield.

It is not revealed how this weapons carrier ended up on its roof at the bottom of a Saudi Arabian gully during Operation Desert Shield, but the roof is undamaged so it is to be hoped that the crew got out with only minor injuries.

Because of the mobile nature of the Scud launchers, US Green Berets and the British SAS were sent deep into Iraq to find them. The American forces were either on foot, dropped by helicopter or mounted on Humvees. The missiles were launched from an area christened the 'Scud Box' by the Coalition. This was divided into two parts, with the SAS taking 'Scud Alley', south of the Baghdad–Amman road and the Green Berets taking 'Scud Boulevard' to the north. The heavy trucks carrying the Scuds could travel along only the main highways, and this, in open desert country, meant great difficulty for the Special Forces who had to travel in their vehicles close to those highways. There were few, if any, places to hide a Humvee. When a Scud site had been located, the Special Forces had two choices: to call in an air strike or hit it themselves. Mobile launchers were best hit from the cannon mounted on the vehicles, as the launchers would most certainly have moved on by the time an aircraft had been scrambled.

Another problem met by all forces was the weather. It was winter in the desert. Cold winds would blow across, bringing sandstorms, blizzards and the heaviest rain the region had seen for years. When the wind and rain subsided, fog built up. Nevertheless, the Scud threat was countered successfully and no missiles were launched after 24 January.

The Special Forces had, in fact, been sent into Iraq long before the actual air war had begun, taking soil samples to see how well the ground in the southern Iraqi desert could take the weight of heavy vehicles. Reconnaissance teams were then sent out to locate Iraqi positions. During the land war, the teams continued to operate behind enemy lines, disrupting communications and sending back as much intelligence as possible. The US Special Forces involved were the Green Berets, the Navy SEAL (Sea, Air and Land) and the US Air Force Commando Unit. The last was sent in by helicopter on 17 January to destroy the Iraqi air-defence radar.

The Land War

Once Schwarzkopf was satisfied that the Iraqi defence and command systems were rendered all but useless, the next stage of the campaign could begin. Throughout the build-up of Coalition forces, there had been a presence of warships in the Gulf of Arabia, close to the coast of Kuwait. The intention was to tie up as many of Saddam's forces in that area and to convince him that here was where a major seaborne invasion would take place. US Marines wanted to make a landing on Kuwaiti soil, as expected by Iraq, but the time it would take – an estimated ten days – and the cost of clearing the mines, plus the potential casualties ruled this out in the minds of CENTCOM. Besides, the landing zone was adjacent to a natural gas plant which would create problems of its own if hit by shellfire, and there was grave concern for the safety of the civilian population of Kuwait.

However, preparations for a decoy amphibious assault went on through February, with the Iraqi Navy being gradually destroyed by air power, and Iraqi mines were cleared from the waters of the Gulf. Iraqi forces occupied oil platforms firing SAM missiles. American and Kuwaiti naval vessels began attacking and clearing these platforms, and the occupying Iraqi forces retreated. Qaruh Island was thus the first part of Kuwaiti sovereign territory to be liberated.

G-Day

It was now time for the big one. At 4am Kuwaiti time, 24 February 1991, 'the Bear' struck. The 1st and 2nd Marines, the Tiger Division of the 2nd Armoured, accompanied by Saudi and Egyptian and other Arab forces, had already driven across the Saudi–Kuwaiti border towards Kuwait City. While Saddam fell for the decoy invasion force in

the Gulf, Coalition forces had driven at high speed to the west where they crossed the border and would move behind the Iraqi forces dug in on the northern Kuwait border.

The second move would be to the west. The US 82nd Airborne Division, successors to the heroes of Operation *Market Garden* at Arnhem in World War II, drove far west into Iraq to capture the Al Falman airfield at As Salman, accompanied by French Legionnaires. Iraqi resistance was overcome by artillery and Gazelle helicopters armed with HOT anti-tank missiles. The 101st Airborne, who had also taken part in *Market Garden*, went into action in Chinook helicopters, with Humvees slung underneath. They were accompanied by the 3rd Armored Cavalry, the 24th Mechanized Infantry, the 1st and 3rd Armored Infantry, the 1st Infantry Battalion and the British 11th Armoured Division across the Saudi–Iraq border. To the east, Pan Arabian and Saudi forces would cross into Kuwait.

The speed and firepower of the Coalition forces overwhelmed the badly-equipped, poorly-fed and inadequately-supplied Iraqi conscripts dug in in the desert. Indeed, a greater problem than dealing with any casualties was the handling of a huge number of Iraqi prisoners of war.

An M998 cargo/troop carrier converted in the theatre of war to a support vehicle for the US Air Cavalry in Operation Desert Storm.

Three days after the launch of Operation *Desert Storm* Coalition forces surrounded Kuwait City. A major tank battle took place at Kuwait international airport, where the entire Iraqi force of 100 tanks in the region was destroyed. Further north, on the Iraq–Kuwait border, there was a second, much larger battle between Iraq's supposedly élite Republican Guard and American and British armoured divisions. In the face of M1Abrams and Challenger MBTs and allied air attack, the entire Iraqi contingent of 700 ageing Russian tanks was wiped out. The honour of retaking their capital city was given to the Kuwaitis on 27 February and, by 5.00hr local time, President Bush announced an end to the fighting. In just 100 hours the biggest land battle since the end of the Vietnam War had resulted in the expulsion of Saddam Hussein from Kuwait.

Somalia

After defeat in its war with Ethiopia between 1977 and 1978, Somalia's president Said Barre faced the threat of a revolt. To counter it he put clan against clan in a civil war that diverted attention from his own weakening position. In 1992, when Barre's despotic but intrinsically weak regime collapsed as a result of his own intrigue, he was forced out. A fight for power erupted between two main factions, aggravated by clan warfare. The United Nations Operation in Somalia (UNOSOM) was set up to restore stability and to bring relief to the people who were suffering not only from the disturbance of the war but from a severe drought. UN Resolution 746 enabled a technical team to go to the country to try and bring some humanitarian aid. A ceasefire was agreed in March 1992 and UNOSOM began its work.

On the road from Mogadishu to Biadoa, a convoy of white UN trucks carries food supplies for feeding centres throughout Somalia, in direct support of Operation Restore Hope. *This convoy is guarded by a desert-camouflaged M1044 from the US Marine Corps' 2nd Platoon, C Company, 3rd Light Assault Infantry Battalion, based at Twenty-Nine Palms, California. The weapon on the turret is an M-60 machine gun.*

An M1114 at Ram Jolly Firing Range, Kosovo, in 2000.

NATO-led multinational force, called the Implementation Force (IFOR), started its mission in Bosnia on 20 December. At a strength of 60,000 troops, IFOR's task was to separate the Croatian and the Serbian forces in Bosnia. They would move the opponents' heavy weapons to approved sites, patrol a 1,400km (870 mile) border between the two opposing forces, repair roads and bridges destroyed during the fighting and reopen the Sarajevo airport. Once these had been achieved, IFOR could begin work to restore normality to the lives of the people, allowing elections to take place in Bosnia in September 1996.

From IFOR to SFOR

One week after the elections, NATO defence ministers met in Bergen to assess how the organization might continue the peacekeeping work when IFOR's mandate ended in December. In November and December 1996 NATO foreign and defence ministers concluded that a reduced, two-year military presence was needed to provide the stability necessary to consolidate the peace. They agreed that NATO would organize a Stabilization Force (SFOR), to begin immediately IFOR's mandate ended.

SFOR had a NATO-led, unified command under the political direction and control of the Alliance's North Atlantic Council, as stipulated by the Peace Agreement (Annex 1A). NATO's Supreme Allied Commander Europe (SACEUR) had overall military authority over SFOR. With 32,000 troops from thirty-three nations as diverse as the USA, Russia, the United Kingdom, Spain, Morocco, Lithuania, Albania and Argentina stationed in Bosnia and Herzegovina, the task of SFOR was to prevent hostilities from flaring up, to promote a climate in which peace could grow and also, where possible, to provide selective support to civilian organizations.

Russian forces had joined IFOR in January 1996 and the First Russian Separate Airborne Brigade stayed on with SFOR's American-led Multinational Division (North). The participation of Russia shows how the former antagonists of NATO and the Warsaw Pact could now work together successfully in the cause of peace.

SFOR worked to support the UN High Commission for Refugees (UNHCR) in its supervising tasks for the return of refugees. A zone of separation was set up, and returns to it were negotiated among the parties to the Peace Agreement and others directly concerned. SFOR helped to facilitate returns, including making sure that no weapons other than SFOR's were brought back into the zone of separation.

KFOR and Kosovo

Situated in southern Serbia, Kosovo has a mixed population, the majority of whom are ethnic Albanians. Within the former Yugoslavia, Kosovo enjoyed a high degree of autonomy until 1989, when Milosevic brought it under the direct control of Belgrade. This was a move that was opposed by the Kosovar Albanians and, in 1998, in fighting between Serbian military and police forces and Kosovar Albanian forces, over 1,500 Kosovar Albanians died and 400,000 were forced from their homes. Milosevic paid no heed to diplomatic efforts to resolve the crisis. On 28 May 1998 NATO set out two major objectives with respect to the crisis in Kosovo: these were to help to achieve a peaceful resolution of the crisis by contributing to the response of the international community, and to promote stability and security in neighbouring countries, with particular emphasis on Albania and the former Yugoslav republic of Macedonia.

On 13 October 1998, as the situation deteriorated, the NATO Council authorized air strikes. This was to support diplomatic efforts to make Milosevic withdraw from Kosovo, to end the violence and to allow the refugees to return. Eventually Milosevic agreed to comply and the threat of air strikes was called off. However, Milosevic

continued to defy attempts to halt his ethnic cleansing and a seventy-seven-day air campaign lasting until 10 June 1999 was conducted to force him to stop his activities.

A multinational force, KFOR, with some 50,000 troops, was set up to oversee the withdrawal of Serb troops from Kosovo, which was completed by 20 June. KFOR was at the forefront of the humanitarian efforts to relieve the suffering of the Kosovar refugees forced to flee by Serbian ethnic cleansing. This was achieved by building refugee camps, refugee reception centres and emergency feeding stations, as well as moving many hundreds of tons of humanitarian aid to those in need.

As a result of the atrocities committed by the Bosnian Serb forces during the Kosovo campaign, Milosevic was charged with war crimes under the Geneva Convention and in February 2002 was put on trial at a specially convened court in The Hague.

A Testimony to the Humvee

Whatever is said about any piece of military equipment by historians, enthusiasts or collectors, no opinion of it is as well qualified as that by someone who has used it in combat. Here is one man's opinion of his Humvee, that of a US Special Forces DMV (Desert Mobility Vehicle) commander who served in the Gulf War and in Somalia:

I will give a ringing endorsement for the HMMWV! It was totally reliable, extremely rugged, exceptionally powerful, and carried everything we needed. Five men could very easily live out of a DMV in comfort – plenty of room for 'lickies and chewies!' It was a stable platform for the .50 cal as well as the Mk19 40mm auto grenade launcher. It would go anywhere. On the downside, it has no legroom whatsoever, and if you don't have the nice bucket seats that we had in our DMVs, it is very uncomfortable during long movements. And the top hatch of the weapons carrier leaks like a sieve in the rain – thank God it doesn't rain much in the places we usually worked!

9   The Civilian Hummer

Ex-military vehicles have always found some sort of market, either as cheap, powerful workhorses, or, latterly, as leisure vehicles or preservation projects. During World War II many American servicemen wrote to their government asking whether jeeps would be sold off when the war was won or whether they would be made in a civilian version. Some wanted a jeep for work; for their farm or ranch, or in construction work, while some wanted a vehicle for leisure, to take them into the backwoods, for hunting and fishing. Ward Canaday of Willys-Overland had already been working on a civilian model, and the customers got it in 1946 in the form of the CJ-2A.

As far back as 1948 jeep fans started a passion for off-roading with the DeAnza Jeep Cavalcade in California. As other vehicle manufacturers got

into the market, the 4×4 vehicle became an essential tool for anyone spending time working or playing off the beaten track. As time went by and Americans began to earn more money and have more leisure time, they began buying 4×4s purely for sport, as tow trucks or as safe vehicles for adverse weather conditions.

Although the Humvee had been in existence since 1985, it was the television coverage of the Gulf War in early 1991 that brought it to the public's attention. The film actor Arnold Schwarzenneger wanted one badly and so contacted AM General. They advised him at first that they were not prepared to sell any to civilians: the vehicle was not EPA-compliant since the military had a long-standing exemption. Schwarzenneger persisted and, in due course, the company sold

The auto writer Ed Mroz takes the wheel during the Hollister Heights trial. Mroz would write a report of the test for Soldier of Fortune *magazine.*

A photo opportunity at Hollister Heights. The four civilian models, the four-door soft top, two-door pick-up, four-door pick-up and four-door wagon pose with a military Humvee.

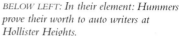

BELOW LEFT: In their element: Hummers prove their worth to auto writers at Hollister Heights.

him a converted weapons carrier. Then, realizing its potential, AM General investigated the possibility of producing a civilian Humvee. They were extremely quick to produce test models, which were given to members of the motoring press in May 1991 to evaluate at Hollister Hills Park off-road testing grounds, central California. Here, over the sort of going used to test military vehicles, the testers found just how well it could perform. One of the most remarkable things they discovered was how easy the Humvee, now given its registered civilian tag of the Hummer, was to drive. Its size suggested that it was a brute, but with power steering, power brakes and a fully automatic transmission, the Hummer needed only a light touch, and, with its high ground clearance, wide track and low centre of gravity, it showed more than enough capability to leave the civilian market off-road 4×4s for dead.

Once they decided to build a civilian Hummer, AM General put it through CHAT (the Civilian Hummer Accelerated Test). This was a condensed test that put a considerable number of miles on the test vehicles, over test tracks, any and all rough going, and on the highway, to establish what kind of mileage they would do before anything broke or wore out. A military vehicle in peacetime does far fewer miles than a civilian

The dashboard of the military Humvee used on the Hollister Heights trials. Compare it with the picture of the production moulded dash on page 126.

truck over a given period. CHAT was undertaken to satisfy the demands of fleet users such as construction engineers, fire departments, oil-field contractors and forest rangers. A commercial user would know from established data just how much it would cost to run, say, a GMC truck in comparison with an International, but no such data for the Hummer existed before CHAT.

Another task that AM General needed to undertake was the establishment of a dealer network. As we have seen, the company was once a part of American Motors, who had a national dealership network selling both their passenger cars and Jeeps; but AM General had been sold off in 1983 to LTV who had no involvement with the civilian auto industry whatsoever. In any case,

The 6.2ltr diesel engine in the civilian Hummer test vehicle.

Pre-production civilian Hummer, with Kevlar doors from the military weapons carrier, instead of the production side-impact protection doors. The lights, which comply with EPA regulations for Class III trucks, are different from those on military models, but are not entirely the same as those that would be found on production versions. The turn indicators/sidelight units would be replaced by square indicators. The bonnet moulding is the same as on the military vehicle and highlights the absence of the black-out light.

AMC had been bought by Chrysler in 1987. AM General had to do what everyone told them was impossible: build a dealer network from scratch. It was a steep learning curve, but the key was to find dealers who understood the nature of this unique vehicle. There were many who thought they did, but AM General were quite firm about whom they chose.

The data established by CHAT would be essential for dealers in selling the Hummer, once those dealers were signed up. And, once established, the location of some of the most successful dealers is sometimes surprising. They are not necessarily found where the hills and the badlands are, but where the money is. The Hummer, after all, is not a cheap vehicle. California became the biggest market; Florida would be big, as would New York State and New Jersey. But the single biggest dealer in the USA would turn out to be in St Louis, Missouri.

The big selling point of the Hummer was that it would do everything the military vehicle would do. At the end of 1992 the first production civilian model came off the line at South Bend. Five basic body styles were built: two- or four-door pick-ups, each available with hard or soft top, equivalent to the M998 cargo/troop carrier. A new style was added too: a four-door, hard-top station wagon.

Although the general mechanical specifications remained the same as for its military sibling, the civilian Hummer had to be adapted to meet the stringent Federal Motor Vehicle Standards. Its type and size put the Hummer in the category for Class III trucks. To comply, three-point seat belts, a padded dash, a collapsible steering column and side impact beams were fitted. In short, the regular equipment fitted to any other vehicle of its class on the roads of the USA at the time. The equipment expected on a normal civilian vehicle, but not considered necessary by the military, such as locking doors and keyed ignition, was also included. Bucket seats and easy-clean, plastic, interior trim were added, but the basic body frame was not altered, so space for driver and passengers was as limited as it was in the military model.

The civilian Hummer's off-road capability is no different from that of its military equivalent. Without the deep-water fording kit, shown fitted, it can cross rivers up to 30in (76cm) deep.

Ultra Coach of Corona, California built this remarkable stretch Hummer, a twenty-four-seater with a raised roof, a digital fireplace, red laser light show, wet bar and full sound system. This vehicle, claimed to be the first such on the West Coast, is run by LeGrande Affaire Limousine Service of Santa Clara, California and was booked up for a year ahead as soon as it arrived.

Wibe, the Swedish firm of Wikstrand and Berg, are specialists in telecommunications and lightning masts. They use this Humvee to get to the remote locations of some of their masts.

EZ-Kool glass, heat and sound insulation, halogen headlights, high-back bucket seats, MT tread tyres, 124A alternator, power steering, a sliding rear window on two- and four-door models, a tachometer and a tonneau cover on four-passenger models. Optional equipment included, among other items, the run-flat tyre system, Monsoon Premium audio system with CD player/changer, heated windscreen, highway touring tyres, driveline protection and a brush guard. The four-door wagon sold from $94,529 and had as standard vertical rear doors, power door-locks on all doors, heat and sound insulation and power windows.

The range for 2002 was cut down to a four-door wagon and four-door soft top, with a CD changer/audio tape player and a heated windscreen as standard on the hard top. There was something in the offing – an all new Hummer.

The HUMMER H2

In January 2000 GM and AM General announced that they would expand the production capacity for a new derivative to be made alongside the original model. While AM General would continue to make the HMMWV for military use, the new product would be jointly developed with General Motors. That vehicle, a 'vision concept' coded H2, was unveiled at the Detroit auto show in January 2000.

'From Notion to Motion in a Matter of Weeks' was the motivation for the vehicle's design and engineering team who started work in late August 1999. The task was to make a civilized, driver-friendly HUMMER without losing any of the vehicle's inherent toughness and off-road capabilities. Once the team had defined what the owners could choose, in theory, between the five basic types. However, Humvees offered for sale by the military would more often than not be in the basic M998/M1038 cargo/troop carrier form. Finding, for instance, hard roofs, Kevlar or supplemental armour doors, shelters, ambulance bodies and armaments carrier slantbacks is possible, but at present these parts can be expensive and not easy to find. Pioneer tools, camouflage netting and weapons may also be found.

Getting About with a Humvee

It is by no means unusual for military vehicles to be transported to military vehicle shows by transporter by virtue of their size or because a tracked armoured vehicle is not suitable for use on public roads. The Humvee may be driven on public roads: some of the few in the United Kingdom are and some are trailered. But however they get to the show, they do attract a great deal of interest. All but a few are in the M1998/M1038 configuration while at least two are fitted out as weapons carriers. At the time of writing, no ambulance nor shelter carrier variants are known to be in Britain.

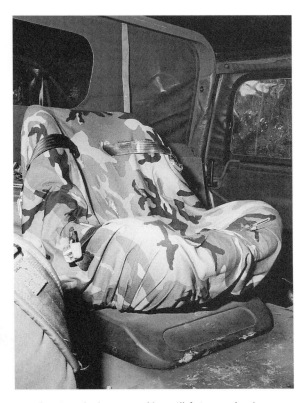

But if you're only three years old, you'll fit in anywhere!

…but not so much in the back!

ABOVE: *If a brush guard is fitted it must be lowered before the bonnet is opened.*

The front suspension is easily accessible once the bonnet is open.

ABOVE: The doors are easily removable – just unhitch the webbing check-strap and lift them off the hinges.

The cargo bed is 52in (132cm) wide between the wheel arches. The chassis is literally just under the bed, which accounts for the height.

The high level of noise generated by the earlier diesel engines, which exceeds 85dBA in the passenger compartment of the M1097 and the M1097A1 and A2 is well known to the US military, who have a requirement for the driver and passengers of these vehicles to wear hearing protection when their engines are running. Certainly they are as noisy to ride in as an older diesel truck. However, if you are concerned about the noise, the provision of simple ear defenders is not a problem. Coupled with the noise, the distance between the driver and the front passenger caused by the drivetrain cover does make the Humvee a less than sociable vehicle, nor is it the best vehicle in which to appreciate a good in-car stereo.

Although they are easy to drive, the great width of the Humvee means that it is not the most suitable of vehicles for the narrower roads of Britain. In fact, driving it will give the impression of filling the entire lane of an A-class road. And, since their performance could not be described as 'sparkling', you may meet with some degree of dissatisfaction from other road users who might be following you – not an unusual occurrence for the drivers of older commercial or military vehicles. Nevertheless, their rarity always attracts attention. If you drive one you will always find someone who will want to ask you questions. They will either be people who have no idea what the vehicle is or those who know something about it and want to know more.

Civilian Hummers

If Humvees are not cheap, then civilian Hummers are definitely in the top price bracket. A good example in the United Kingdom will fetch somewhere in the region of £45,000. However, the current British Driver and Vehicle Licensing Agency (DVLA) regulations would seem to prevent the personal importing of a Hummer. It is the weight of the vehicle that, as a general rule, provides the apparent reason for its exclusion.

The DVLA's Criteria for Type Approval for Personal Import (PI) state that PI status does not apply to HGVs with a GVW over 3,500kg (3.15 tons). The Hummer's GVW is 4,671kg (4.20 tons). Appendix 2 of the Department of Transport, Local Government and the Regions' booklet SVA4 *The Single Vehicle Approval Scheme* (SVA) states that:

One of two Hummers available for hire from Specialist Leisure Ltd. It makes an unusual wedding vehicle.

Very rare is this right-hand-drive model, borne out of a venture to sell Hummers in Australia. It is shown here on Black Rock Sands, near Portmadoc, North Wales. Note the different side-light arrangement to comply with British law.

... if a heavy goods vehicle is of the same 'family of types' that has already passed SVA (either as a goods vehicle no more than 3,500kg gross weight, or as a passenger car) it may be submitted for SVA providing:

The design gross weight does not exceed 5,500kg [4.95 tons]; and,

The kerbside (i.e., unladen) weight does not exceed 3,425kg [3.08 tons].

These vehicle weights are long-standing: they have been agreed by the UN Economic Commission for Europe and the European Union as the point at which goods vehicles become 'heavy' and, most significantly, should have different safety standards.

The document goes on to define 'family of types' as vehicles which do not differ in the manufacturer, the essential aspects of design and construction, the chassis/floorpan and the powerplant. This particular rule dates from August 2001 and is a relaxation of the previous one that demanded that all HGVs over 3,500kg needed to be fully type-approved according to European Community regulations.

The SVA scheme uses low-cost tests designed predominantly for 'personal use' vehicles and is thus restricted to private vehicles. HGVs over 3,500kg GVW must be type-approved, but the Goods Vehicle National Type Approval scheme does offer an opening for the would-be personal Hummer importer in that individual vehicles can be catered for. Anyone applying for an exemption should

point out that the GVW of the original M998 is just below the GVW limit, at 3,493kg (3.14 tons) and below the specified kerb weight, at 2,359kg (2.12 tons). The civilian Hummer is a member of the same vehicle family as the M998 – it is made on exactly the same production line and moved only to a different paint and trim shop. Therefore it may be argued that the Hummer should be allowed into Britain under SVA as a family member of a vehicle that is of a GVW below the limit. However, the question of having a bespoke SVA scheme for heavy goods vehicles might be addressed as part of the European Commission's proposals to extend mandatory EC Whole Vehicle Type Approval to HGV classes, so anything may happen up to and beyond 2003.

The extreme rarity of the vehicles gives them some exclusivity; but their owners are generally not prone to any snobbishness. In fact, most are quite happy to talk to those genuinely interested in the vehicles. And, if you cannot get your hands on the real thing, there is plenty of merchandise to buy and a select few available for hire. Specialist Leisure, a company based in Yorkshire, handles American 'Hummer Stuff', including designer clothing, key rings, mugs, compasses and scale models. They have two Hummers, both four-door Wagons, one red and one white, for hire for special occasions.

If you chose to buy a Hummer or a Humvee you will be, for the next few years at least, a member of a very select club.

Appendix I
Model Identification at-a-Glance

The American armed forces used the Humvee in many variants, from the basic M998 cargo/troop carrier to the armoured M1116. Here each model is listed by variant and number.

Variant	Original No.	First Upgrade	Second Upgrade
cargo/troop carrier	M998	M998A1	
cargo/troop carrier w/winch	M1038	M1038A1	
heavy variant	M1097	M1097A1	M1097A2
TOW carrier, armoured	M966	M966A1	
TOW carrier, armoured w/winch	M1036		
TOW carrier, supplementary armour	M1045	M1045A1	M1045A2
TOW carrier, supplementary armour w/winch	M1046	M1046A1	
armament carrier, armoured	M1025	M1025A1	M1025A2
armament carrier, armoured w/winch	M1026	M1026A1	
armament carrier, supplementary armour (USMC exclusive)	M1043	M1043A1	M1043A2
armament carrier, supplementary armour w/winch (USMC exclusive)	M1044	M1044A1	
S250 shelter carrier	M1037		
S250 shelter carrier w/winch	M1042		
ambulance, 2-litter, armoured (mini)	M996	M996A1	
ambulance, 4-litter, armoured (maxi)	M997	M997A1	M997A2
ambulance, 2-litter, soft top	M1035	M1035A1	M1035A2
expanded capacity vehicle	M1113		
fully armoured weapons carrier	M1114		
fully armoured TOW missile carrier (not produced)	M1115		
fully armoured weapons carrier (USAF exclusive)	M1116		

Notes
USMC: US Marine Corps
USAF: US Air Force
Not all variants were upgraded to A1 or A2 status
Ambulance variants: when the M998A1 variant was introduced, the ambulance variants were uprated, with the exception of the M996 mini ambulance, which was discontinued. The newer variants simply used the existing numbers with A1 or A2 added, according to engine and suspension specification
Variants based on the expanded capacity vehicle were not classified with the regular A1/A2 upgrades, having exclusive running gear.

Appendix II
Abbreviations

ATCCS   advanced tactical command and control System

BLAAM   bunkers, light armour and masonry

CECOM   Central Command (US Army)

CENTCOM   Central Command (Gulf War)

CHAT   civilian Hummer accelerated test

COHHV   cab-over heavy Hummer variant

COHSE   cab-over Hummer special equipment

COMBATT   commercially-based tactical truck

CTIS   central tyre inflation system

CUCV   commercial utility cargo vehicle

DARPA   Defense Advanced Research Projects Agency

DMV   desert mobility vehicle

DT/OT   durability test/operating test

ECV   expanded capacity vehicle

EOD   explosive ordnance

EPA   Environmental Protection Agency

FMC   Food Machinery and Chemical Corporation

FOT&E   follow-on test and evaluation

GDLS   General Dynamics Land Systems

GEP   General Engineering Products Division of AM General

GFPU   gas particulate filter unit

GM, GMC   General Motors, General Motors Corporation

HE   high explosive

HEAT   high explosive anti-tank

HHV   heavy Hummer variant

HMMWV   high mobility multipurpose wheeled vehicle

HVAC   heat, ventilation and air-conditioning

IFOR   Implementation Force

KFOR   Kosovo Force

LAPES   low-altitude parachute extraction system

LMS   lightweight multi-purpose shelter

LRV   light reconnaissance vehicle

LSRV   light surveillance and reconnaissance vehicle

MMBMF   mean miles between mission failure

NATC   Nevada Auto Test Center

NBC   nuclear, biological and chemical

NDAC   National Defense Advisory Commission

OCO-D   Office, Chief of Ordnance, Detroit

OTAC   Ordnance Tank Automotive Center

RAM-D   reliability, availability, maintainability and durability

SFOR   Stabilization Force

SICPS   standardized integrated command post system

TACOM   Tank-Automotive Command, Tank-Automotive and Armaments Command

TARDEC   Tank Automotive Research, Development and Engineering Center

THAAD   theatre high-altitude air defense

TOW   tube-launched, optically sighted, wire-guided (missile system)

TRADOC   Training and Doctrine Command

UNHCR   United Nations High Commission for Refugees

UNMIH   United Nations Mission in Haiti

UNOSOM   United Nations Operations in Somalia

UNPROFOR   United Nations Protection Force

USAFE   United States Air Force, Europe

WHEELS   US military special analysis of wheeled vehicles (operating between February 1972 and April 1973)

Index